FOUNDATIONS OF MUSIC
A Computer-Assisted Introduction

ROBERT NELSON AND CARL J. CHRISTENSEN

For Apple II© Series
DISKETTE INCLUDED

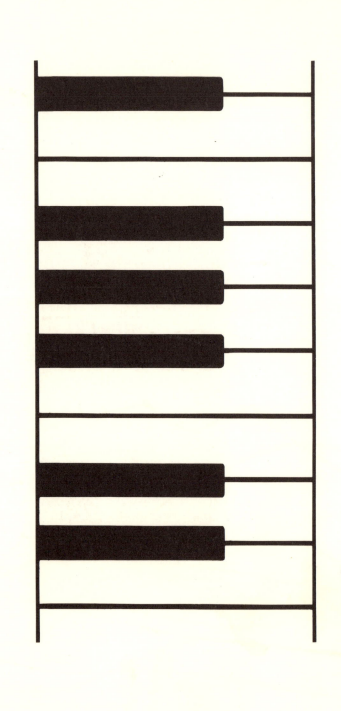

FOUNDATIONS OF MUSIC

MUSIC BOOKS OF RELATED INTEREST

Leon Dallin, *Foundations in Music Theory with Programmed Exercises*, 2d Edition
William Duckworth, *Creative Approach to Music Fundamentals*, 2d Edition
Neil McKay/Marion McKay, *Fundamentals of Western Music*
Gary Martin, *Basic Concepts in Music*, 2d Edition
William Duckworth/Edward Brown, *Theoretical Foundations of Music*
Elie Siegmeister, *Harmony and Melody, Volumes I and II*
William Thomson, *Introduction to Music Reading*, 2d Edition
William Toutant, *Functional Harmony, Volumes I and II*
Carolynn Lindeman, *Pianolab*
Charles Lindsley, *Fundamentals of Singing for Voice Classes*
Helene Robinson, *Basic Piano for Adults*
Royal Stanton, *Steps to Singing for Voice Classes*, 3d Edition

FOUNDATIONS OF MUSIC

A Computer-Assisted Introduction

Robert Nelson
University of Houston

Carl J. Christensen
Hartnell College

Wadsworth Publishing Company
Belmont, California
A Division of Wadsworth, Inc.

Music Editor: Sheryl Fullerton
Editorial Assistant: Cynthia Haus
Production Editor: Deborah O. McDaniel
Designer: Andrew H. Ogus
Print Buyer: Barbara Britton
Copy Editor: Hinda Farber
Autographer: Ernie Mansfield
Compositor: G&S Typesetters, Inc.
Cover photograph courtesy of Apple Computer, Inc.

SOFTWARE ACKNOWLEDGMENTS

The routine that erases portions of the high resolution graphics screen was written by Vernon C. Noble, who also provided invaluable assistance in both musical and programming matters.

The sound generation routine was written by S. Scott Zimmerman.

This disk contains a high-speed operating system called Diversi-DOS™, which is licensed for use with this program only. To legally use Diversi-DOS with other programs, you may send $30 directly to: DSR, Inc., 34880 Bunker Hill, Farmington, MI 48018-2728. You will receive a Diversi-DOS disk with documentation.

Apple is a registered trademark of Apple Computer, Inc. DOS 3.3 © 1980–81, Apple Computer, Inc.

Printed in the United States of America

1 2 3 4 5 6 7 8 9 10—91 90 89 88 87

Library of Congress Cataloging-in-Publication Data

Nelson, Robert, 1941–
    Foundations of music.

    Includes index.
    1. Music—Theory—Computer-assisted instruction.
I. Christensen, Carl J., 1945–.   II. Title.
MT6.N225F7   1987   781   86-13193
ISBN 0-534-06894-4

CONTENTS

PREFACE

"I WANT TO LEARN ABOUT MUSIC!"

This is a fair enough request and one commonly heard on college campuses. The student may be motivated by nothing more than the desire to fulfill a fine arts requirement in a painless way, but our experience has taught us that the student is just as likely to have some prior experience with music—playing in a "garage" band, taking a few piano lessons long ago—or just enjoys listening to music and genuinely wants to know more about it. In each case, the student hopes that a course or two in music will increase his or her understanding and thereby enhance and deepen his or her musical experiences.

Unless such students elect to major in music, in all likelihood their choice will be either a music "appreciation" course or a course in music fundamentals. This may be supplemented with beginning study in piano or some other instrument. This book is intended for use in music fundamentals classes for non–music majors at the college level, but could also be used successfully at the advanced high school level, or as a supplement to first year theory for college-level music majors. It should also integrate nicely with any methods for beginning instruments.

Realistically, the number of hours that nonmajors can devote to fine arts is limited. Given this fact, any fine arts course—broadly defined—should provide some overview of the subject matter, impart useful facts or skills, and ultimately provide the critical bases for a greater understanding that one hopes will lead to greater enjoyment and broadened tastes.

"THIS IS A MAJOR SCALE. SO WHAT?"

Those of us in music have, at some time, endured a great deal of drudgery in learning our scales and key signatures. We take it for granted that this is important. But students at the college level will be coming from a much different frame of reference.

• They may know nothing about music—only that you listen to it.

• They may play by ear, but are unable to express verbally what they are doing, much less write it down. Yet they may really be quite musically intuitive.

• They may have a smattering of knowledge of scales and key signatures and very likely knowledge of a few chords.

What they all want (and need) is to be able to deal with notated music as they encounter it in sheet music, songbooks, hymnals, or their elementary piano music.

It seems to us that too many rudiments books present only the raw material of music without going that one step further and presenting a clear and simple context within which the student can see the operation, and in fact the very rationale, for the materials being studied.

Our attempt is to present rudiments holistically—by always relating the fundamentals being studied to actual musical practice through copious musical examples. These examples have been carefully graded for comprehension, and questions for guided discussion have been included throughout. This approach has proven successful at more advanced levels, and we feel that it actually stimulates the learning process.

Musical examples have been chosen from a wide variety of historical periods and genres, including popular music. The intent has been to move from examples that are familiar to those less well known.

"THAT SOUNDS NICE. WHAT IS IT?"

Musical literacy involves two complementary skills—reading and writing—and exercises for both are found throughout the book. But above all, perhaps, music involves listening skills. One applies "book knowledge" to an aural experience, and in that aspect music is unlike any other art form. Consequently, the importance of looking and listening to actual music virtually from the outset cannot be overstated. Suggested Listening assignments have been included where new topics are introduced. In many respects, students can *hear* concepts prior to their being able to *read* and understand them. And it is always worthwhile to relate the aural experience to the actual study of the musical concept at hand. The listening examples should, of course, be discussed. As with the printed examples, the goal has been breadth of style and idiom. All the pieces cited are standard repertory and should be readily available on records.

"At Last! My Own (Digital) Tutor!"

There's no escaping the fact that fluency in music requires a sure and thorough acquaintance with key signatures, the various forms of scales, intervals, and the like. Music teachers know from long experience that these topics can only really be absorbed by drill and repetition—the same techniques so indispensable to learning basic arithmetic or spelling.

Up to now, this has meant both a large investment in class time—leaving less time for more musical pursuits—and a necessary redundancy in the amount and types of writing and recognition drills. We feel that "programmed" texts have been largely unsatisfactory. First, the student must use the frames "honestly"—that is, he or she must do all of them, in order, and not peek. Second, the frames never change, in effect limiting the amount of variety and redundancy in the problems. Third, and most important, "programmed" texts cannot by their very nature deal with the intangibles one finds in even the simplest piece of music.

Our book deals with the problem by incorporating computer-assisted exercises. The advantages of using the computer are manifold:

• Drill and practice are made more enjoyable. Almost all students report that the interactive audio-visual aspect of the computer makes learning more fun.

• The interactive nature of the exercises helps the student learn as a participant rather than as a mere observer. There is very little flashcard-style drill. Rather the student is asked to add measure lines, complete measures, add accidentals, or spell chords.

• Study can be truly self-paced. Since each computer exercise drills a very specific topic with a small number of problems presented repeatedly but in a random order, a student may do as few or as many repetitions as necessary.

• The computer provides instant correction. The student does not have to wait several days for homework to be returned to find out if the work was done correctly.

• The computer can actually play the music notated on the screen. Scale and chord-spelling exercises take on a whole new relevance when the student can listen to the effect of accidentals as they are added.

• The computer can give special help in the area of rhythm. We include rhythm programs in which the student taps the displayed rhythm on the keyboard. The computer evaluates the performance and displays the student's version if it is incorrect. The computer then plays the correct version.

• All of the programs can be used on a standard Apple II series computer with one disk drive and a monitor. There is no need to buy expensive add-ons.

• Finally, all of this happens in a private, uncritical environment. The computer is a tireless tutor with infinite patience!

At the same time, we feel that the computer, while a versatile and useful tool, cannot replace the teacher in the classroom. This is particularly true when dealing with the subtleties of the actual music. For best results, the teacher should present the material in class, utilizing as completely as possible the Suggested Listening examples and the musical examples printed in the book. The latter should be sung or played in class. Chord symbols are in many cases supplied, so that guitar or autoharp can be used—along with piano—for accompaniment.

Wherever the symbol for the computer-assisted instruction appears, the student should go to the computer and drill on the given materials. The computer-assisted instruction is designed for individual pacing, instant grading, and correction as needed; it can also provide a log of exercises attempted and the cumulative score. The computer drills are user friendly, in that no prior experience with a computer is required. The teacher may want to begin with a group session with the computer to allay the fears of those students not so technologically inclined.

Written exercises may be assigned at the teacher's discretion. These exercises develop writing skills and are intended to complement the work on the computer.

Class time saved should be devoted to a listening to and discussion of Music for Study sections. Every attempt has been made to supply a breadth of style and idioms, but the teacher may wish to have students bring in their own examples—particularly pop music.

A cautionary note: music is never as crystal clear as we might like. There will always be a few ambiguities. Encourage the students to ask questions. At some point, the complete answer to their questions might be further study in music theory. Remember, as a teacher you will be opening doors. Give them a sure footing in the basics, and then wish them a *bon voyage* as they go on exploring the many worlds of music.

We would like to acknowledge the following people for their aid and encouragement in the preparation of this book:

Joy Nelson, California State University, Fresno; Herbert Bielawa, San Francisco State University; Robert Placek, University of Georgia; and Alan Stanek, Idaho State University, for their assistance in reviewing the manuscript;

Vernon C. Noble and Dr. Frederick Lesemann for their review of the software;

Sheryl Fullerton and Debbie McDaniel of Wadsworth for their many valuable editorial suggestions, and for their shepherding of the book from its initial conception to its final form;

Our many students who helped test our materials and offered many helpful suggestions.

Our gratitude to Carl Mann for proofing the typescript and to the indefatigable Margaux Mann for her countless hours slaving over a hot word processor.

Lastly, a special thanks to Carole and JoAnn for supporting us in so many ways during the development of this book.

USE OF THE COMPUTER

THE FLEXIBLE DISK that comes with this book contains the computer-assisted instruction materials referred to in the text. These materials are designed primarily for individual use by students, but instructors may find it useful to run the programs on a large monitor for an entire class to demonstrate the musical concepts discussed in the text.

This disk may be used on any of the family of Apple II computers that has at least 48K of memory. Since the program writes your score on the disk and since disk drive speeds may vary, try, if possible, to always use the same machine.

Treat the disk with care. Always store it in its protective envelope, do not bend it, and handle it only by the label end. Do not subject it to magnetic fields or extremes of heat or cold.

When the indication for computer-assisted instruction appears in the text, merely insert the disk, label side up, in drive one, close the drive door, and turn the computer and monitor on.

The first time the disk is used, you will be asked to type your name. Since your progress through the material will be recorded on the disk, it is important that it be customized in this manner. At the beginning of each subsequent session, you will be asked to enter your name in exactly the same form.

After typing your name, the disk drive will run for a while and then the main menu will appear. This menu looks exactly like the table of contents for the text. It is called a menu because you make selections from it. Notice that each indication for computer-assisted instruction in the text guides you to a given chapter and topic, and then asks you to do a specific drill. Follow this path by making the appropriate selection from each menu as it appears.

When you finish a drill, you may return to the main menu by pressing the ESCAPE key (ESC).

1

The main menu also allows you to view the record of your progress. You may even produce a printed copy of your records if you have access to a computer with a printer attached. Your instructor may ask you to turn in this printout as evidence of your independent study.

To end a study session, continue to press the ESC key until you return to the main menu. Then select the END option by pressing E. The disk drive will run for a few seconds and your progress will be recorded on the disk. *Wait for the computer to tell you when to remove the disk and turn off the power.* Always use this method to end a study session before you turn the computer off.

Sometimes you will be asked to turn the disk over. Be sure to wait until the drive light goes off before doing this and to close the drive door after reinserting the disk.

Do not be afraid of the computer. There is no danger of pressing a "wrong" key. If an irrelevant key is pressed, the computer will respond with two short beeps. The only key to avoid is RESET. Always check to see that the CAPS LOCK is down. If a program stops running (crashes), press the left arrow several times, then press RETURN several times, and finally type RUN and press RETURN. If the program still will not run, turn the computer off for a few seconds and turn it on again.

You will notice that while doing the exercises, you may seek help by typing "?". This will return you to the instructions for help with the mechanics of the exercise. If you need help with the material, consult the text or your instructor.

Do not be afraid to make mistakes. In almost all of the exercises, you will be given several chances to modify your answer.

Finally, it is very important to do a significant number of repetitions (at least twenty in most cases) in each section of each computer exercise. Concepts that are explained in a few short paragraphs in the text may require an extended session of drill and practice to really master. The authors are confident that the computer-assisted materials will provide an enjoyable and effective means of attaining this mastery.

Computer-Assisted Instruction: Contents and Log

USE THIS LOG to note the exercises assigned by your instructor. The indications in the column on the right—(1a), (2x), etc.—may be used to identify specific levels of an exercise. You may want to record the number of problems that you have done on each exercise. This information will also be recorded on the disk if you finish each session with the END option from the main menu.

CHAPTER 3   SOUND

There are no drills for this chapter.

CHAPTER 4   SCALES

WHOLE STEPS AND HALF STEPS

THE MAJOR SCALE

CHAPTER 5   INTERVALS

2. Interval Spelling

Seconds and Thirds only

    Construct Intervals
ABOVE Given Note   (5i) ——————————————

    Construct Intervals BE-
LOW Given Note   (5j) ——————————————

Major, Minor and Perfect Intervals only

    Construct Intervals
ABOVE Given Note   (5k) ——————————————

    Construct Intervals BE-
LOW Given Note   (5l) ——————————————

Sevenths only

    Construct Intervals
ABOVE Given Note   (5m) ——————————————

    Construct Intervals BE-
LOW Given Note   (5n) ——————————————

All Qualities of Simple
Intervals

    Construct Intervals
ABOVE Given Note   (5o) ——————————————

    Construct Intervals BE-
LOW Given Note   (5p) ——————————————

3. Interval Recognition

Seconds and Thirds only   (5q) ——————————————

Major, Minor and Perfect Intervals only   (5r) ——————————————

Sevenths only   (5s) ——————————————

All Qualities of Simple
Intervals   (5t) ——————————————

4. Inversion of Intervals   (5u) ——————————————

5. Compound Interval
Recognition   (5v) ——————————————

CHAPTER 6   CHORDS AND HARMONY

1. Triad Writing
   Major and Minor Triads   (6a)   _____
   Major, Minor and Dimin-
   ished Triads   (6b)   _____
   All Types of Triads   (6c)   _____

2. Triad Spelling
   Major and Minor Triads   (6d)   _____
   Major, Minor and Dimin-
   ished Triads   (6e)   _____
   All Types of Triads   (6f)   _____

3. Triad Recognition
   Major and Minor Triads   (6g)   _____
   Major, Minor and Dimin-
   ished Triads   (6h)   _____
   All Types of Triads   (6i)   _____

4. Dominant Seventh Writing   (6j)   _____

5. Dominant Seventh Spelling   (6k)   _____

6. Dominant Seventh
   Recognition   (6l)   _____

7. Chord Recognition   (6m)   _____

CHAPTER 7   SIMPLE FORMS

There are no drills for this chapter.

CHAPTER 8   LOOKING AT MUSIC

1. Musical Terms
   Dynamic Indications   (7a)   _____
   Tempo Indications   (7b)   _____
   Character and Expression
   Indications   (7c)   _____

INTRODUCTION

SUGGESTED
LISTENING Listen to short examples from a wide variety of sources. Include classical music from several periods, popular music, show tunes, even folk music and music from other cultures, if desired. The class may wish to submit examples from their own collections. In discussion, consider the following:

1. What do all the examples have in common? What common properties (such as *sound* and *time*) are in evidence?

2. What differentiates the examples? What gives each piece its unique characteristics? Is the music simple or complex? How many performers seem to be involved?

3. How does the music affect your emotions or feelings? To what general musical characteristics might you be reacting?

Don't be concerned with using any musical terms for the time being. Rather, describe your sensations very generally.

In times past, a cultivated person was expected to have some first-hand familiarity with one of the fine arts, whether painting, music, drama, or literature. And while some few aspired to be what in our day would be called professionals, many others avidly became amateurs—in the original meaning of "lovers of the arts," rather than in the sometimes demeaning or pejorative sense. The key was certainly active rather than passive participation.

Today we are more than likely "consumers" of the arts—audience rather than participant. While we still value the concept of cultural "refinement," we must often be content with a few "appreciation" courses in college, or season's tickets to the symphony or theater. And though we wouldn't deny that even passive involvement in the arts is a positive thing, many of us still regret at one time or another that we didn't stay with those piano lessons, or that we never got around to *really* learning the guitar, or that we never knew the pleasure of gathering around the parlor piano for an old-fashioned song fest.

No matter. Perhaps it's never too late—at least to enjoy music first hand, whether as a player or a singer or just a listener. But as with so many other endeavors, the more we know about something, the more enjoyment we derive from it. This is all the more true with music, which has its own peculiar and largely symbolic language.

What is offered in this book is the fundamentals of musical literacy. This is a primer, if you will—the grammar of the musical language. Reading this book and doing the exercises will *not* make you an instant performer or composer! But it should open doors—doors to enhanced appreciation of all the music around you, and doors that beckon to a friendlier world of actual *doing*, by unlocking the mysteries of musical notation and thus of music itself.

This book follows the traditional progression from the rudiments—note values, pitch notation, scales, and key signatures—through intervals and chord structures to a preliminary treatment of phrase structure and musical form. Throughout the book, as much music as possible has been incorporated. In the early sections, your comprehension may be minimal; but rather than being discouraged, you should instead measure your growth by the increase in understanding as you master each successive level.

As in many other endeavors, certain achievements come only with repetitions. Such is the case with our rudiments. To lighten this sometime chore, the drill exercises have been put on a computer disk. This allows you to spend whatever time is necessary to master each item. It also has the virtue of providing instant correction, and thus enhances the speed at which you develop true fluency.

The importance of this fluency cannot be understated. Since the material is cumulative, no new material should be attempted until each drill has been thoroughly mastered. And while reading the book is certainly necessary, *just* reading the book will not be sufficient.

Lastly, we must stress that musical literacy is, strictly speaking, not a goal in itself but a means to a greater end. One obviously doesn't sit down and "read" a piece of music as one does a short story or novel. Music is intended to be played or, of course, listened to. And while this book concentrates on reading and writing skills, it should prove a useful adjunct or complement to classes in piano, recorders, guitars, or other instruments.

At the same time, you are encouraged to sing or play as many of the musical examples as your level of skill will allow. Many of the musical illustrations have been chosen for familiarity or accessibility. A simple system of numbers or syllables might well be used to reinforce the theoretical concepts with practical reading skills. Many of the melodies have been provided with chord symbols not solely for the study of harmony but for the in-class use of guitar or autoharp. The guiding philosophy throughout has been to progress from the familiar to the unfamiliar, from simple to more complex.

This book is but a first step in the study of music. The topics of harmony and form are far too broad and complex for adequate treatment here. It is hoped that with a sound fundamental training, you will be able to go on to a more detailed and specialized study. At the very least, it is hoped that this book will both enrich your musical experience and encourage a continuing lively curiosity about all matters musical.

One

THE NOTATIONAL SYSTEM

MUSIC IN WESTERN CULTURE

The culture of any society is measured in large degree by the richness of its arts—poetry, painting, and music among them. Music in particular seems to fulfill a most basic human creative impulse and so appears early on in a civilization's development. Music is the logical accompaniment to ritual; whether religion or magic or pure wonder, music has been used to express those thoughts and feelings that transcend the mere verbal.

The exact form and expression that music takes vary from culture to culture. Some find their highest expression in song and develop it to a high degree of sophistication; other cultures aspire to symphonies.

The comparative study of the music of different cultures is called *ethnomusicology* and is a fascinating study. Unfortunately, in this book we must concentrate on just one small area—Western music from roughly the end of the seventeenth century to our own day. Western music is principally that of Western-European culture; we will have occasion to touch only briefly on other cultures, in those specific instances of influence or cross-fertilization.

One of the glories of any culture is that sense of common heritage. Regardless of our nationality or language, we can share in works of art. Beethoven was German, but was known all over Europe in his own day. In our day, his works are played and enjoyed worldwide. Musical ideas travel freely and know no borders; our contemporary star performers from concert pianists to pop singers are internationally known. Music is truly a universal language.

WRITTEN MUSIC

Let's follow that last thought a bit further. If we want to read a novel by Thomas Mann in its original language, we must know German; similarly, if we wish to read Voltaire untranslated, we must know French. But once we know the mechanics of music notation we can just as easily read a piece of music by Brahms (Austrian) or by Debussy (French) or Mussorgsky (Russian). It's all the same, at least as far as the notes themselves go.

We can be thankful for that, but we must also appreciate the fact that it might not be so. Certainly, a system of notation, while useful, is not absolutely necessary. Most primitive cultures get along nicely without it and certain traditions—those we generally call folk art—still rely on aural transmission and are stored, so to speak, in the people's collective memory. Much of popular music and jazz is largely improvised or uses so-called head arrangements, and is only later transcribed into written form.

Well, why have a written tradition then? You are probably familiar with what happens to a rumor as it gets spread around. It often comes back in considerably altered form. The same is true of music handed down by aural tradition. Each generation "remembers" slightly differently, and each performer is free to add embellishments. Thus, no *absolute* version of a folksong can be said to exist. This works reasonably well with folksongs, but problems arise when the music becomes more complex.

Historically, the impetus toward notation was supplied by our Western penchant for **polyphony**—the combining of several melodic lines simultaneously. In order for this to be successful, the several parts must be coordinated, and the lines must stay reasonably the same every time. A system of notation provides a close if not exact means of indicating the composer's intentions. Once established, it allows an unprecedented expansion of musical expression in form, content, and length. Imagine trying to teach a chorus and orchestra even one chorus of Handel's *Messiah* by *rote*, that is by singing each and every part until the performer had it memorized! Instead, with music notation we have a record of how Handel himself actually conceived the piece, and we can reproduce and enjoy that creation for centuries to come.

MUSIC—A TEMPORAL ART

We said above that music notation was a close but not exact representation of the actual music. Why this is so becomes clearer if we consider the unique nature of music.

Music is, first of all, *sound*. Music is intended to be heard. This may seem a strange statement in a book about reading and writing music, but we must never forget that notation is only a means of getting the music from the composer to the listener, by way of the performer. We can describe sounds in a number of general but useful ways. We say that sounds are high, or low, or somewhere in the middle. This aspect of sound is called **pitch.** Or we can say that sounds have different colors or intensities. This aspect is called **timbre** (pronounced *tam*ber). We say that sounds are loud or soft. This aspect is known as **dynamics.** When single pitches occur in succession, the result is **melody;** several pitches occurring simultaneously result in **harmony** or **chord** structures.

Lastly, all sounds from the most simple to the highly complex have *duration*, that is to say, they last only a certain amount of time, varying from a fraction of a second to several minutes. When the music stops, it is gone in the physical sense and remains only in our memory. You can't leisurely observe a symphony in the same way you can observe a piece of sculpture or a painting. You *can* study a **score**—the written version—of a symphony, but that can never really be the same as hearing the symphony. Like drama, our enjoyment of a piece of music relies on our remembering what we have heard and relating that to current and subsequent musical events. Music is a *temporal* art form, and it follows that the devices for organizing musical time are very important. These devices come under the general heading of **rhythm,** and will be discussed in detail in the next chapter.

Translating these often complex combinations of sounds and durations into a system of symbols is no small accomplishment. Our system of notation has evolved somewhat willy-nilly over the centuries and is still changing and adapting to meet the ever-changing nature of the music itself. But no matter how sophisticated the notation, there are still *interpretive* decisions that are left to the performer. It is interesting to hear how much two performances of the same piece can differ—even when played by the same performer! Music notation is not unlike a map or key; it is but a guide to the ultimate re-creation of a work of art.

NOTES AND RESTS

Any notation system, then, consists of symbols that represent specific aspects of the sound we hear—principally pitch and duration. These symbols are given names, so that we can verbalize the manifold relationships that exist among the sound events themselves.

The basic symbol is the **note.** By using several different but related symbols, we can represent varying but mathematically related values.

All sounds have specific durations from quite short to very long. Typically, in any piece of music there will be a variety of durations, and one set of symbols must be flexible enough to indicate these durations with reasonable precision. The note with the largest value that is still commonly used is the whole note, an oval shape (called the **notehead**) that is slightly tilted: 𝅝 . There is a value called a double whole note (also occasionally called a breve), which is written either as a bracketed whole note or as a square note:

‖𝅝‖   𝆩

This note is no longer in common use.

Other values are derived by a process of simple binary division. A whole note divides into two half notes: 𝅗𝅥 𝅗𝅥. The half note is the same oval head with a **stem** attached. The stem may go up or down depending upon context.*
Observe on which side of the head the stem is attached in each case. Two half notes equal one whole note in value.

𝅗𝅥 + 𝅗𝅥 = 𝅝

Half notes are divided into quarter notes: 𝅘𝅥 𝅘𝅥. Here the notehead is filled in. Two quarter notes equal one half note; four quarters equal one whole note.

𝅘𝅥 + 𝅘𝅥 = 𝅗𝅥 ,   𝅘𝅥 + 𝅘𝅥 + 𝅘𝅥 + 𝅘𝅥 = 𝅝

Quarter notes are divided into eighth notes: 𝅘𝅥𝅮 𝅘𝅥𝅮. The curved line to the right is called a **flag**. Notice that it always goes to the right.

Eighth notes are divided into sixteenth notes 𝅘𝅥𝅯, sixteenths into thirty-second notes 𝅘𝅥𝅰, and so on, simply adding additional flags. With groups of flagged notes, the flags may be replaced with a single **beam**:

𝅘𝅥𝅮 𝅘𝅥𝅮 = 𝅘𝅥𝅮𝅘𝅥𝅮   𝅘𝅥𝅯 𝅘𝅥𝅯 𝅘𝅥𝅯 = 𝅘𝅥𝅯𝅘𝅥𝅯𝅘𝅥𝅯

For every note value, there is a companion symbol that is used to represent a duration of silence. These symbols are called **rests.** As we will see,

---

*See page 26.

rests "count" just as much as the notes themselves. Here are the common rests along with their relative values:

whole rest    or

half rest    or

quarter rest

eighth rest

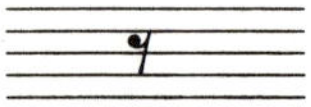

sixteenth rest

thirty-second rest

We now have a basic set of symbols. Additional values can be notated by using the dot and the tie. Placing a **dot** after the notehead adds *half* the value of the note:

Rests may also be dotted:

A second dot adds half the value of the first dot.

A dotted note can, of course, be divided into three equal values. Additionally, a dotted note can be divided into two equal values, each of which will itself be a dotted note.

A **tie** joins the values of two or more notes* into one longer value:

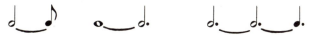

Up to this point we have defined durations only in relationship to other durations (for example, a quarter note is half as long as a half note). The actual length of notes in clock time will take us into a discussion of the way musical time is organized, which we will cover in the next unit.

CHAPTER 1   THE NOTATIONAL SYSTEM

RHYTHM NOTATION

  1. NOTE VALUES (NAMES & EQUIVALENTS)
  2. NOTE VALUES (INCLUDING DOTS & TIES)—ALL LEVELS
  3. RESTS—ALL LEVELS

WRITTEN
EXERCISES

Once you have mastered the computer drills, work out the following exercises. It is important to master the skills of both reading and *writing* music, and it may take some practice before your notes and rests appear uniform.

1. Identify the indicated note parts:

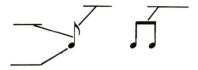

2. On the line below, write the indicated values. Take care to place the noteheads squarely on the line. Stems may go in either direction in this instance, but should be positioned on the correct side of the notehead and perpendicular to the horizontal line, not leaning. Draw the

---

*In Chapter 3, we will encounter a similar curved line called a **slur**. The difference in the two is this: the tie will always connect notes of the *same* pitch, while the slur will be used to group notes of varying pitches. (See page 81.)

flags neatly and with care. The flags should be curved around to meet the stem.

a.   half note   b.   eighth note   c.   quarter note   d.   sixteenth note

e.   dotted quarter note

3.   Duration equivalents: Indicate the number of notes of a given value that it would take to equal a second value. For example: __2__ ♩ = 𝅗𝅥

a.
___ ♩ = 𝅗𝅥   ___ ♪ = ♪
___ ♪ = 𝅗𝅥   ___ 𝅘𝅥𝅯 = 𝅘𝅥𝅯
___ 𝅘𝅥𝅯 = 𝅗𝅥   ___ 𝅘𝅥𝅯 = ♪
___ 𝅘𝅥𝅰 = 𝅗𝅥   ___ ♪ = 𝅗𝅥
___ 𝅗𝅥 = 𝅝   ___ 𝅘𝅥𝅯 = ♩
___ ♩ = 𝅝   ___ ♪ = 𝅝

b.
___ ♩ = 𝅗𝅥.   ___ 𝅗𝅥. = 𝅗𝅥.
___ ♪ = 𝅗𝅥.   ___ ♪. = 𝅗𝅥.
___ ♪ = 𝅗𝅥.   ___ 𝅘𝅥𝅯 = 𝅗𝅥.
___ 𝅘𝅥𝅯 = ♪.   ___ ♪ = 𝅗𝅥.
___ ♩ = 𝅝.   ___ 𝅗𝅥. = 𝅝.

c.
___ ♩ = 𝅝 ⌣ 𝅗𝅥   ___ ♪ = 𝅗𝅥 ⌣ 𝅗𝅥.
___ ♩ = 𝅗𝅥 ⌣ 𝅗𝅥   ___ ♪ = 𝅗𝅥. ⌣ 𝅗𝅥 ⌣ ♪
___ ♪ = 𝅗𝅥 ⌣ ♪   ___ ♪ = ♩ ⌣ 𝅗𝅥 ⌣ ♪
___ ♪ = 𝅗𝅥. ⌣ ♩   ___ ♩ = 𝅝 ⌣ 𝅝 ⌣ 𝅗𝅥.

4. On the line below, write the indicated rests. Center the rests on the line. Observe whether the rest sits *on* the line (half rest) or *under* the line (whole rest).

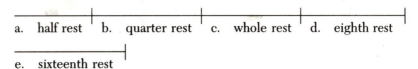

   a. half rest   b. quarter rest   c. whole rest   d. eighth rest

   e. sixteenth rest

5. Duration equivalents using rests:

LETTER-NAMES FOR NOTES

Pitch notation requires a means of designating the individual sounds and differentiating their relative highness or lowness, or, as we say, their **register**. For names, we use the first seven letters of the alphabet, A through G, which are cyclically repeated. Why this is so will become clear when we discuss sound in greater detail.

For pitch notation, our now-familiar note shapes are placed on a **staff**. A staff consists of five parallel lines and the spaces in between. For reference, lines and spaces are numbered from the bottom up.

The specific letter-names for notes on the lines and spaces are established by **clef** signs. There are three clefs in common use: treble or G clef, bass or F clef, and C clef. As the names suggest, each clef fixes a certain pitch letter-name on a certain staff line.

The treble clef is in fact a highly modified script G. Note the similarity:

The curlicue at the base of the clef denotes the second line as G.

All the other lines and spaces now have pitch letter-names:

There are many clever mnemonic devices for remembering the lines: *Every Good Boy Deserves Favor*, for example. You may know some others. If not, it might be fun to invent some new ones.

The treble clef is used for higher sounds, such as those produced by violins, flutes, and the upper register of the piano. The word *treble* originally designated a high voice.

The bass clef is likewise a modified script F:

When placed on a staff, it denotes the fourth line as F:

As a result, the lines and spaces in bass clef have different names. You can remember the lines with: *Good Boys Do Fine Always*; and the spaces with: *All Cows Eat Grass.*

This can be confusing at first, but learning to read music requires knowing both clefs and being able to keep them distinct. With practice, both will become quite familiar to you.

The bass clef is used for lower sounds, such as those produced by trombones, tubas, cellos, string basses, men's voices, and the lower registers of the piano.

The spaces above and below the staff are routinely used, and the staff can be extended by the use of **ledger lines,** small lines the width of a notehead that in effect continue the lines of the staff:

However, use of more than four ledger lines can make reading difficult. Pitches lying even higher or lower can be indicated by the symbol *8va*, which stands for *octava* (Italian for octave). The root stem of *octave* translates as *eight*. We find that the letter-name eight degrees away from any pitch is the same:

A	B	C	D	E	F	G	A
1	2	3	4	5	6	7	8

As we will see, all pitches having the same letter-name are in a sense equivalent; it is the same pitch but in a higher or lower register. So these two notes are equivalent:

but the first one is easier to read. *8va* can be used to indicate very low pitches as well, and the *8va* is written under the notes:

The C clef denotes a given line as the letter C. Unlike the G and F clefs, the C clef is movable and may designate the third line as C (alto clef):

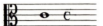

or the fourth line as C (tenor clef):

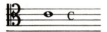

C clefs are used by mid-range instruments such as violas, which routinely read in alto clef. Cellos, trombones, and bassoons use the tenor clef when the music falls in their upper registers. Use of the appropriate clef allows most of the music to be notated on the staff, eliminating the cumbersome necessity of using many ledger lines.

This gives us a complete system for indicating precisely the relative highness or lowness of any pitch. Within a given clef, the higher the symbol *appears* on the staff, the higher will be the actual sound.

The following convention is observed for notes having stems: If the note lies below the third line the stem goes up; if the note lies on or above the third line, the stem goes down.

Where a group of beamed notes appears, the stem direction is governed by where the majority of the notes lie.

Single staves are routinely used for the voice parts of songs and for individual instruments, where the total range from low to high can be accommodated. In situations where the pitches cover a very wide range, as with the piano, a treble and bass clef are combined into a **great** or **grand staff:**

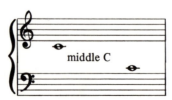
middle C

The two staves have a nice symmetry. Note the placement of the indicated C. This C is known as **middle C,** and in a sense comes right between the two staves. Because of the distance between the two staves, however, this C must be placed closer to one staff or the other, as in the illustration. Ledger lines can be used above and below either of the staves, though for practical reasons fewer are used in between the staves. Typically, lines will simply pass from one staff to the other:

Lines passing from clef to clef may necessitate some adjustments in stem direction within beamed groups:

For vocal or instrumental ensembles, several staves may be braced together into a **system.**

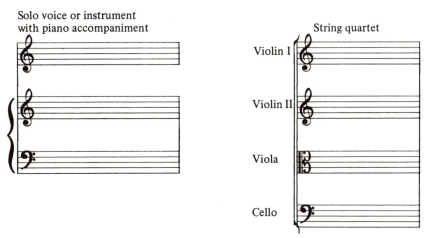

CHAPTER 1   THE NOTATIONAL SYSTEM

PITCH NOTATION

    4.   PITCH NAMING—ALL LEVELS (TENOR & ALTO CLEFS OPTIONAL)

    5.   PITCH WRITING—ALL LEVELS (TENOR & ALTO CLEFS OPTIONAL)

REGISTERS OF THE PIANO

For ease in reference, the gamut of pitches (illustrated here with the piano keyboard) is divided into specific registers, each consisting of seven pitches from C to B. Following is the range of the piano, notated conventionally on a great staff, with the appropriate registral designations and the system of letter designations:

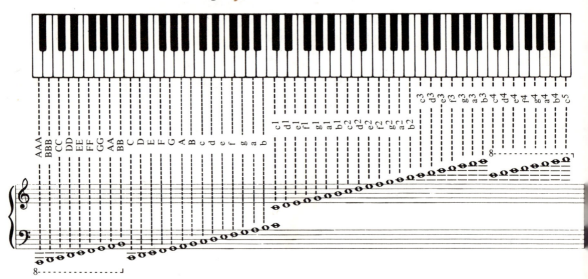

CHAPTER 1   THE NOTATIONAL SYSTEM

PITCH NOTATION

    6.   PIANO KEYBOARD

WRITTEN EXERCISES   As before, after mastering the computer drills, work out the following written exercises.

    1.   Write the letter-name for each of the following pitches, using the correct registral designations:

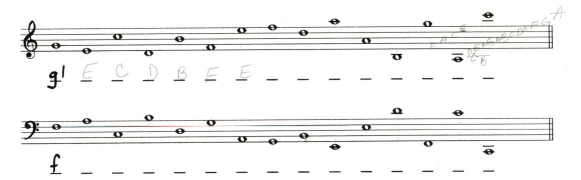

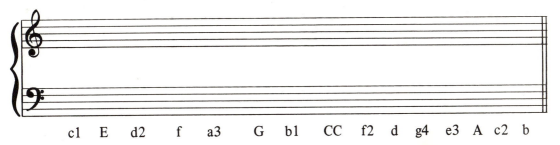

2. Write the notes indicated by the letter-names at the appropriate place on the great staff. Use ledger lines or *8va* as needed. Take care that the noteheads are placed clearly on the appropriate line or in the appropriate space.

c1   E   d2   f   a3   G   b1   CC   f2   d   g4   e3   A   c2   b

3. Rewrite this melody in bass clef in the register indicated by the first note. Stem directions may need to be changed, depending on where the notes fall on the staff. Be sure the stems go on the correct side of the note. Whenever writing music, work for neatness, clarity, and legibility.

4.   Rewrite this melody in treble clef, following the directions for exercise
     3 above. Register is indicated by the first note.

Two
RHYTHM AND METER

SUGGESTED
LISTENING

Listen to several selections of music designed for movement, such as marches or dance music. These may be drawn from a wide spectrum of periods and styles, including the latest in popular music. Notice your physical response to the music. What characteristics of the music elicit this response? Do you react especially to any particular instruments or any particular element in the music? As before, don't be concerned if your responses are very general.

THE BEAT

Rhythm is the most basic element of music. It is hard to conceive of music that is pitches only, with *no* sense of rhythm whatever, but we can easily imagine rhythms without pitches. In fact, we can recognize many pieces just by their rhythmic patterns alone, and it follows that rhythm is an important element in making music memorable.

When listening to a piece of music, notice your physical reaction to the rhythm. If you are like most people, you will end up tapping your foot, or otherwise moving in time to the music. You are responding to the *beat* of the music.

We define the **beat** as a series of pulses or segments of musical time that are even, regular, and ongoing. The beat is a reference point for all the varied durations of the notes. The beat is something we feel, though in some cases it may be made quite explicit. (When you listen to the drums in a marching band or jazz band, the bass drum likely will be playing the beat.)

The durations of the sounds themselves may be equivalent to the value of the beat; they may be several beats long; or there may be several notes to

31

each beat. We tend to feel the beat as the value somewhere between the slowest (i.e. longest) notes and the shortest. Since this is a psychological response, individuals may differ in their perception of the beat. We will observe also that the speed or pace of the beat varies from piece to piece. The rate of the beat is called **tempo** and is indicated either by reference to a metronome or by terms describing the speed or character of the piece. We will encounter these terms shortly.

Finally, we can designate any note value as the unit of the beat, even dotted note values. A given note achieves a specific duration only when the number and tempo of the underlying beats is established.

Now, music consisting of only beat-length values would be fairly dull; likewise, too wide a variety of different durations will soon begin to sound incoherent. What is needed is a rational and perceivable organizational scheme for relating and understanding (as well as limiting) the variety of durations presented by any piece of music. This structural scheme we call **meter.**

The Organization of Music into Meters

If we tap or clap an extended series of beats at a moderate tempo, we begin to notice a subconscious tendency to differentiate or organize the beats into patterns marked by regularly recurring accent or stress. These will generally follow one of two possibilities—every other beat or every third beat accented. We may feel these accented beats as stronger or subtly louder. It would be like writing the notes as follows:

If we then separate these patterns by vertical lines, we have a series of **measures** or **bars** of two or three beats each:

The dividing lines are naturally called **barlines.** Our term *meter*, in fact, comes from the Greek word meaning *to measure.*

This metric pattern then becomes the basis for organizing the rhythms or varied durations of the piece. As a convenience, we indicate the meter or accent pattern to be used by a **meter signature,** which we place at the beginning of the piece.

A metric pattern having two quarter notes to the measure is indicated by the signature $\frac{2}{4}$. The top number tells us the number of beats in the measure, and the bottom number stands for the unit of the beat, in this case a quarter note.* A metric pattern with three quarter notes per measure would be $\frac{3}{4}$. Note that this is *not* a fraction; ¾ is incorrect.

Both $\frac{2}{4}$ and $\frac{3}{4}$ are examples of **simple meters.** In simple meters, note values are routinely combined or divided in multiples of two. The following combinations are typical:

There is really an extraordinary diversity of rhythmic patterns here. Almost any combination of note values is possible, as long as the values within the measure add up to the value indicated by the meter signature. In actual practice, the composer tends to limit the number and complexity of the patterns in any given piece.

Usually, when eighth notes and smaller values are used within a beat they are beamed together. This makes the music easier to read. Individual flags are used only in vocal music where a note takes a single syllable of the text. Dotted notes can be used, but must not obscure the basic meter. In the following example, the written notation is read as if the dot substitutes for the tie:

written: read:

Meters having four beats to the measure are also commonly found. In a sense, one measure of $\frac{4}{4}$ is not unlike two measures of $\frac{2}{4}$, though a subtle distinction is sometimes made between beat one (primary accent) and beat three (secondary accent). (In most music written before about 1750, the first and third beats are generally considered as equivalent.) All the combinations of $\frac{2}{4}$ are found in $\frac{4}{4}$, with these additionally:

---

*This is sometimes notated like this: $\overset{2}{\textbf{\large .}}$

Since any note value can be designated the unit of the beat, we have a large number of possible meters. For sake of easy comparison, we group them by the number of beats:

simple duple: $\frac{2}{2}$ or ¢, $\frac{2}{4}$, $\frac{2}{8}$, $\frac{2}{16}$, etc.

simple triple: $\frac{3}{2}$, $\frac{3}{4}$, $\frac{3}{8}$, $\frac{3}{16}$, etc.

simple quadruple: $\frac{4}{2}$, $\frac{4}{4}$ or C, $\frac{4}{8}$, etc.

Remember, a lower number of 2 stands for a half note, 4 for a quarter note, 8 for an eighth note, and so on. The symbols C and ¢ are a holdover from an earlier system of meter signatures. ¢ means *alla breve*, and designates the half note as the unit of the beat; C is often incorrectly taken to stand for "common" time, but is interchangeable with $\frac{4}{4}$. It is also theoretically possible to have the whole note as the unit of the beat, e.g. $\frac{4}{1}$.

CHAPTER 2   RHYTHM AND METER

SIMPLE METERS

    1. INSERTING BARLINES—SIMPLE METERS—ALL LEVELS

    2. COMPLETING MEASURES—SIMPLE METERS—ALL LEVELS

Ends of sections within a larger composition, and occasionally shorter subdivisions, are set off by the use of a double barline: ‖. This is a means of musical "punctuation." The very end of a composition is indicated by the use of a double barline having one thin and one thick barline: ‖.

WRITTEN EXERCISES Add barlines in the appropriate places for the given meter signature. Place a double barline at the end of each example. The first note or rest is always the first beat of the measure.

Rhythm in Performance

Selecting the proper tempo for a piece of music can be quite subjective. Until the invention of the metronome, tempo was generally determined by the average note value (lots of "fast" notes implied a fast tempo) or by some designation as to the character of the piece (e.g., a dance movement or march or lament). Some of these terms, such as *allegro*, which in the Italian means lively or merrily, now have commonly understood connotations of tempo—in this case, fast. Other examples include *grave*, which means serious or somber and implies a slow tempo, and *largo*, meaning broad or wide, again implying a slow tempo. Other terms were gradually adopted that had more to do with the pace of the beat: *andante*, from the Italian *andare* (to go), which means literally a "walking" tempo; *moderato* (moderately, thus neither slow nor fast); *presto* (very quickly); *tempo guisto* (in exact time), and so forth.

Here are the most common terms, ordered from slowest to fastest. Others will be found in the Glossary.

grave—seriously; thus a slow, solemn tempo

adagio—slower than andante; quite slow

andante—walking tempo; usually interpreted as slow

andantino—literally, a little andante; faster than andante

moderato—moderately; neither too fast nor too slow

allegretto—literally, a little allegro; slower than allegro

allegro—bright and cheerful, thus a fairly quick tempo

vivace—lively; a very quick tempo

The metronome allowed the composer to indicate tempos exactly in relation to clock time by specifying so many beats per minute. For example, M.M. (standing for Maelzel's Metronome) 60 means that 60 beats should occur in a minute's time; M.M. 96 means 96 beats per minute; M.M. 136 means 136 beats per minute.

Experience tells us that it is very difficult to maintain an absolutely precise tempo throughout a piece. As the music gets more exciting, we tend to speed up a little, and as it relaxes we slow down. Composers can indicate a flexibility of tempo by the use of the term **rubato,** which literally means to rob from the time by now holding back and then speeding to "catch up."

The composer may wish to markedly change the tempo. The term *accelerando* (abbreviated *accel.*) means to speed up; *ritard* (abbreviated *rit.*) means to slow down. *Poco a poco* (literally little by little) means gradually. A *tempo* signifies the resumption of a steady tempo following any tempo fluctuation.

This next computer exercise covers some of these terms and introduces some new terms. If you aren't familiar with all the terms, review their definitions in the Glossary.

CHAPTER 8   LOOKING AT MUSIC
   1.   MUSICAL TERMS—LEVEL 2—TEMPO INDICATIONS

COUNTING TIME IN SIMPLE METERS

Sometimes it must seem that musicians spend the greatest part of their lives counting. Counting is the surest way we have of establishing the durational relationships of the notes and performing them evenly and correctly.

There are numerous counting systems, all of which supply a verbal equivalent for each metric unit. We count the beats by number:

one two three four   one two three four   etc.

For notes of several beats' duration, we vocalize the count only where notes occur, but we must keep the beat going to assure precision and uniformity in the note values. We can do this by tapping or clapping the pulse while vocalizing, or we can conduct the metric pattern.

one   three one   three one two three   one

tap:

Simple divisions can be done most simply thus:

one and two and   one and two and   etc.

Subdivisions can be counted like this:

one-e and-a two-e and-a

Here is an example fully counted:

one   two   three   one   and three   one two and-a three-e and one

tap:

The first beat of every measure is called the **downbeat.** This term derives from the conductor's beat pattern, in which the motion for beat one is always straight down. The remaining beats in the measure, and particularly the last beat, are called **upbeats.** It is not at all unusual for rhythmic patterns to begin on an upbeat. A partial measure prior to the first downbeat is called an **anacrusis** or simply a **pickup;** it may be as short as a fraction of a beat or as long as three beats, depending on the meter. One standard convention says that the value of this upbeat is deducted from the final measure (making that measure incomplete), but this convention is not always rigorously followed.

Here are some examples of rhythmic patterns beginning with upbeats or anacruses:

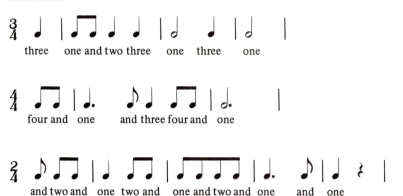

three   one and two three   one   three   one

four and   one   and three four and   one

and two and   one two and   one and two and one   and   one

CHAPTER 2   RHYTHM AND METER

SIMPLE METERS

   3. PLAYING PRACTICE—SIMPLE METERS

      LEVEL 1—VALUES OF ONE BEAT OR MORE

      LEVEL 2—SUBDIVISIONS

MUSIC FOR STUDY

Write out and count the rhythms of each of the following melodies. Identify the meter of each. How many beats in a measure? What is the unit of the beat? (You will find any unfamiliar tempo terms defined in the Glossary at the end of the book.) First, count the rhythms aloud, using a neutral pitch. Then, count along as the tune is played or sung.

EXAMPLE 1.   "PASSING BY"
Traditional

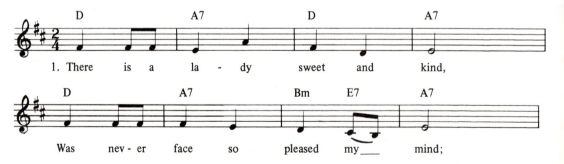

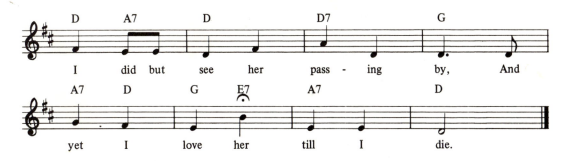

I did but see her pass - ing by, And yet I love her till I die.

EXAMPLE 2.   SYMPHONY NO. 7, SECOND MOVEMENT
             Ludwig Beethoven (1770–1827)

Allegretto

EXAMPLE 3.   "FOLLOW THE LEADER"
             Bela Bartók (1881–1945)

Allegretto

poco rit.

EXAMPLE 4.   "THE ASH GROVE"
             Welsh Folksong

The ash grove how__ grace - ful, how plain - ly__ 'tis__ speak - ing; The wind thro'__ it__ play - ing has lan - guage for me.

EXAMPLE 5.   "POLOVETZIAN DANCE"
Alexander Borodin (1833–1887)

EXAMPLE 6.   "DECK THE HALL"
Old Welsh Air

Deck the halls with boughs of hol - ly, Fa la la la la la la la la.

'Tis the sea - son to be jol - ly, Fa la la la la la la la la.

Don we now our gay ap - par - el, Fa la la la la la la la la la.

Troll the an - cient Yule - tide car - ol, Fa la la la la la la la la.

EXAMPLE 7.   "THE MERRY FARMER"
Robert Schumann (1810–1856)

Allegro animato

EXAMPLE 8.   SONATINA, OP. 36, NO. 1, RONDO
Muzio Clementi (1752–1832)

EXAMPLE 9.   "AVE MARIA"
Charles Gounod (1818–1893)

EXAMPLE 10.   "DIXIE"
Daniel Emmett (1815–1904)

I__ wish I was_ in the land of cot - ton, Old times there are

not for-got ten, Look a - way! Look a - way! Look a - way! Dix - ie Land.

MUSIC FOR STUDY: COUNTING WITH RESTS   We have observed that the beat is felt to continue steadily under the music, regardless of the actual note values being used, even when the beat is only very subtly implied. In fact, so strong is the sense of the beat, we feel it even during brief stretches where there is no sound at all. It follows that rests must be counted as strictly as the notes themselves:

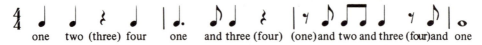

one   two (three) four   one   and three (four) (one)and two and three (four)and one

Count the rhythms in the following melodies. As before, first just count, using a neutral pitch. Then, count along as the melodies are played or sung. Tap the beat to assure rhythmic accuracy with the rests.

EXAMPLE 1.   "SPRINGTIME SONG"
Bela Bartók (1881–1945)

Andante

EXAMPLE 2.   SARABANDE
George Frederick Handel (1685–1759)

EXAMPLE 3.   LITTLE PRELUDE NO. 1
Johann Sebastian Bach (1685–1750)

EXAMPLE 4. AIR
George Frederick Handel (1685–1759)

Rests are also used simply to shorten the value of notes coming on the beat. Here the rests would not be counted, strictly speaking, but would tell the performer to release the note on the second half of each beat.

EXAMPLE 5. "SOLDIER'S MARCH"
Robert Schumann (1810–1856)

Allegro

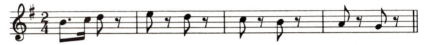

COMPOUND METER

SUGGESTED
LISTENING

Franz von Suppé, *The Light Cavalry Overture*, second theme

Morton Gould, *American Salute*

John Philip Sousa, *Washington Post March*

Nicolai Rimsky-Korsakov, *Sheherazade*, first movement (from m. 18 on); third movement

Meredith Willson, "Seventy-six Trombones" from *The Music Man*

The characteristic lilt of these examples owes to the frequent use of a long-short rhythmic pattern. If we listen carefully, we will find that each beat is divided into three equal parts, and this is what defines a **compound meter.**

A compound meter presents several problems. We know from our earlier discussion that our basic note-value symbols are always divided into *two* of the next smallest value, and we can't divide a note into three parts using any of the standard note values.

There are two possible solutions to this dilemma. First, we can use what we call a **triplet** figure. This is a type of proportional notation that means to play three notes in the time of two. Stated as a ratio, it would be 3 : 2, but we simply use the 3, along with a slur or bracket for unbeamed notes:

However, if an entire piece uses these divisions, the triplet becomes very cumbersome. The second possibility is to work up from the value of the division itself, what we shall call the **background unit.** If we need three background units for every beat, it follows that we can then sum these values into a single *dotted note,* and this value can then be used to represent the beat in compound meters:

(background)   = (beat unit)

(background)   = (beat unit)

But how do we express this in a meter signature? In a simple meter, we can designate the beat unit by a digit: 4 for ♩, 2 for ♩, etc. But a dotted note would become a fractional number: ♩. = 4½(?). We could simply use the note value: $\frac{2}{♩}$ or $\frac{3}{♩.}$. Unfortunately, this has not become standard usage.

Instead, we must represent the background unit in the meter signature. The upper number is then derived by counting the total number of background units:

$= \frac{6}{8}$

The term *compound* implies that we feel subgroups of three, and there is an implied accent pattern within the subgroup:

This is not unlike two measures of $\frac{3}{4}$, and the distinction between the two meters is not always clear. In fact, we often feel the pulse of compound meters at the level of the background unit and even count the music at that level, especially when the tempo is slow. Consider this example:

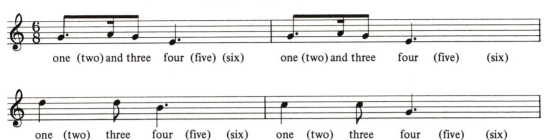

"SILENT NIGHT"
Franz Grüber (1787–1863)

one (two) and three four (five) (six)   one (two) and three   four   (five)   (six)

one (two) three   four (five) (six)   one (two) three   four   (five)   (six)

Compare:

one   and   three   one   one   and   three   one

A quicker example is more easily counted like this:

"THE WILD HORSEMAN"
Robert Schumann (1810–1856)

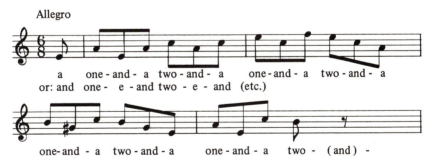

Allegro

a   one - and - a   two - and - a   one - and - a   two - and - a
or: and one - e - and two - e - and (etc.)

one - and - a two - and - a   one - and - a   two - (and) -

The "trick" in counting rhythms is to keep simple and compound meters distinct. Certain patterns are difficult to distinguish clearly and must be counted with care, always mentally keeping the smallest value clear and steady. For example:

think

one-e-and-a two-e-and-a   one-and-a two-and-a

Keep the notes even in value!

Here is another. Do it the same way.

If you find the use of the same vocables for both simple and compound meters confusing, try using this traditional system for counting compound meter:

one - la - le   two - la - le   one-ta - la - ta - le - ta two-ta - la - ta - le - ta

CHAPTER 2   RHYTHM AND METER

COMPOUND METERS

    4. INSERTING BARLINES—COMPOUND METERS—ALL LEVELS
    5. COMPLETING MEASURES—COMPOUND METERS—ALL LEVELS
    6. PLAYING PRACTICE—COMPOUND METERS
        LEVEL 1—VALUES OF ONE BEAT OR MORE
        LEVEL 2—SUBDIVISIONS

WRITTEN
EXERCISES

Add barlines in the appropriate places. Place a double bar at the end of each example. The first note is always on a downbeat.

<table>
<tr><td>MUSIC FOR STUDY; COUNTING COMPOUND METER</td><td>As before, write out and count the rhythms of the following melodies. Identify the meter of each. How many beats in a measure? What is the unit of the beat? What is the background unit? See the Glossary for definitions of the tempo terms. Does it seem more comfortable to count the beat unit or the background unit?</td></tr>
</table>

MUSIC FOR STUDY; COUNTING COMPOUND METER

As before, write out and count the rhythms of the following melodies. Identify the meter of each. How many beats in a measure? What is the unit of the beat? What is the background unit? See the Glossary for definitions of the tempo terms. Does it seem more comfortable to count the beat unit or the background unit?

Here are a few of the most common patterns that you will encounter. Count each of them two ways: first, counting the beat unit, and second, counting the background unit.

EXAMPLE 1.   "SAILING"
Traditional

Lively

Sail - ing,   sail - ing   o -ver the bound - ing main,_____   for

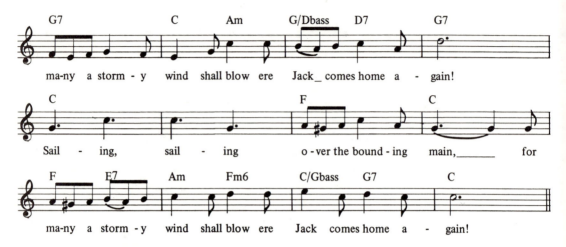

| G7 | | C | Am | G/Dbass | D7 | G7 |

ma-ny a storm-y wind shall blow ere Jack__ comes home a - gain!

| C | | F | C |

Sail - ing, sail - ing o - ver the bound - ing main,_____ for

| F | E7 | Am | Fm6 | C/Gbass | G7 | C |

ma-ny a storm-y wind shall blow ere Jack comes home a - gain!

EXAMPLE 2.   "For He's a Jolly Good Fellow"
Anonymous

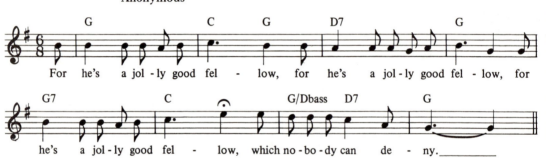

| G | | C | G | D7 | | G |

For he's a jol - ly good fel - low, for he's a jol - ly good fel - low, for

| G7 | | C | | G/Dbass | D7 | G |

he's a jol - ly good fel - low, which no - bo - dy can de - ny._____

EXAMPLE 3.   "When Johnny Comes Marching Home"
Traditional

With spirit

| Gm | | Bb | | Gm |

1. When John-ny comes march-ing home a - gain, Hur - rah,____ hur - rah!___ We'll give him a heart - y

| Bb | | Bb | | F |

wel - come then, Hur - rah,____ hur - rah!___ The_ men will cheer, the boys will shout, The

la - dies, they_ will   all   turn out, And we'll all   feel   gay,   When   John-ny comes marching home.

EXAMPLE 4.   "STILL WIE DIE NACHT"
          Karl Bohm (1844–1920)

EXAMPLE 5.   SONATINA IN G, ROMANZA
          Ludwig Beethoven (1770–1827)

EXAMPLE 6.   SHEHERAZADE
             Nicolai Rimsky-Korsakov (1844–1908)

EXAMPLE 7.   "GYPSY LOVE SONG"
             Victor Herbert (1859–1924)

EXAMPLE 8.   NOCTURNE OP. 9, NO. 2
             Frederick Chopin (1810–1849)

Classification of Meters

In summary, meters are classified first as simple or compound, and then as to the number of beats per measure; meters having two beats per measure are called **duple,** those with three **triple,** and those with four **quadruple.** Meters with the same number of beats, but with a different division, have a strong relationship, and patterns common to one are often found in the other. A common example would be with the meters $\frac{2}{4}$ and $\frac{6}{8}$.

The same rhythmic pattern is notated above first in a simple duple meter, and then in the equivalent compound meter. The **duplet** accomplishes in a compound meter what the triplet accomplishes in a simple meter.

The following excerpt illustrates the concept of equivalent meters very neatly. The first three measures are in compound quadruple meter with ♩. as the beat unit. In measure four, the meter changes to the equivalent *simple* quadruple meter with ♩ as the beat unit. The *tempo* of the beat stays the same, but instead of three notes per beat there are only two, making the eighth notes in effect longer and slower, as you can tell by listening to and counting this example. It's a simple yet very effective device.

Symphony No. 5, Second Movement
Peter Tchaikovsky (1840–1893)

Changes to the equivalent
simple meter (♩. = ♩)

All the common meters along with their classification will be found in the following table. Keep this page handy for reference.

TABLE OF METER SIGNATURES

		Simple			Compound		
		Meter	Beat Unit	Background Unit	Meter	Beat Unit	Background Unit
Duple		2/2 ¢	𝅗𝅥	♩	6/4	𝅗𝅥.	♩
		2/4	♩	♪	6/8	♩.	♪
		2/8	♪	♬	6/16	♪.	♬
		2/16	♬	♬			
Triple		3/2	𝅗𝅥	♩	9/4	𝅗𝅥.	♩
		3/4	♩	♪	9/8	♩.	♪
		3/8	♪	♬	9/16	♪.	♬
		3/16	♬	♬			
Quadruple		4/2	𝅗𝅥	♩	12/4	𝅗𝅥.	♩
		4/4 C	♩	♪	12/8	♩.	♪
		4/8	♪	♬	12/16	♪.	♬
		4/16	♬	♬			

WRITTEN EXERCISES

1. Examine each of the following rhythm patterns. Note whether the smaller values are grouped in twos (indicating a simple meter) or in threes (indicating a compound meter). Count the number of beats. Then, identify the meter of each example. Place the meter signature on the staff, in its appropriate place. In certain instances, there may be two possibilities, such as $\frac{2}{4}$ or $\frac{4}{8}$. Always reduce to one of the common meters listed in the Table of Meter Signatures. (For example, reduce $\frac{8}{8}$ to $\frac{4}{4}$ or $\frac{2}{2}$.)

a.

b.

c.

d.

e.

f.

g.

h.

i.

j.

2. Complete the following chart.

Meter	Classification	Number of Beats	Beat Unit	Background Unit
$\frac{4}{4}$	Simple quadruple	four	♩	♪
1. $\frac{9}{8}$				
2. $\frac{2}{4}$				
3. 𝄴				
4. $\frac{6}{4}$				
5. $\frac{3}{16}$				
6. $\frac{4}{8}$				
7. 𝄵				
8. $\frac{3}{4}$				
9. $\frac{4}{2}$				
10. $\frac{12}{16}$				

THE USE OF BEAMS

We have seen how much of an aid beams can be in recognizing meters. Beams should be used to group any and all small values falling *within* a beat:

In meters like $\frac{2}{4}$, $\frac{3}{4}$, and $\frac{4}{4}$, beams may connect notes of like value from one beat to the next:

You will notice that an entire measure of shorter meters can be combined under one beam, but notes in a "long" meter like $\frac{4}{4}$ are routinely combined in half measures.

Beams should always reflect the meter. Incorrect beaming:

Correct beaming—notice the clarity of the individual beats:

Simple and compound groupings should be kept distinct; that is to say, smaller values should always be beamed in twos or multiples of two in a simple meter, and beamed in threes in a compound meter. In the example below, the same sequence of rhythmic values is beamed first in a compound meter and then in a simple meter. Count each example so you can feel the implied accents.

Often, accent patterns in, say, $\frac{6}{8}$ and $\frac{3}{4}$ will be alternated. This device is called **hemiola** and is characteristic of much Spanish music. You can hear this in such pieces as "America" from Leonard Bernstein's *West Side Story*, or Aaron Copland's *El Salon Mexico*.

WRITTEN
EXERCISES

In the following exercises, replace individual flags with beams wherever possible. Remember the meter signature!

ESTABLISHING METER THROUGH ACCENTS AND PATTERNS

MUSIC FOR STUDY
Review the melodies used for the exercises in counting on pages 38–41 and 47–50. How is the meter of each melody established? On which counts do long notes occur? Short notes? Where the note values are uniform, what other devices seem to give a sense of the meter?

It is somewhat misleading to look at a meter signature and then *see* how the meter is established. We must always bear in mind that music is intended to be *heard* and must be understood without necessary recourse to the notated score. How the composer accomplishes this little feat will be of some interest to us.

Music, unless a single unaccompanied line, is a composite of many rhythmic patterns, all unified and held together by a common beat unit. We describe music as having **texture;** by this we mean the number of individual voices or parts and their relationship, one to another. However different the rhythms of the various parts might be, they all will in some way serve to establish and reinforce the meter. In complex textures, one voice or part will nearly always clearly define the beat unit. This part is frequently the **bass line,** which is the lowest sounding part, and we generally listen for the beat in the bass instruments—string bass, tuba, etc.—or in the drum parts of a jazz or rock band, for example.

Establishment of meter involves both selection from among the possible note values and organization of the chosen durations, so that the listener perceives the pulse or beat and can readily tell which beats are accented or stressed and which are not.

Accent or stress can be established in a number of ways. One way is by actually accenting a note by playing it louder or with a sharp attack. This type of accent is called a **dynamic accent.** Such attacks are indicated by accent marks placed over or under the noteheads: . These and other symbols will come up again in the next chapter. The same thing can be accomplished by having more instruments play on a given beat, or by using a relatively denser combination of pitches.

Another way is by varying durations. Everything being equal, a longer note will be felt to carry an accent. A pattern of durations such as will easily be perceived as a triple meter. An accent by duration is called an **agogic accent.**

Finally, *pattern* plays an important role in establishing meter. This is most obviously the case in accompanimental rhythms to music such as marches and dances.

Let's examine a specific musical example.

TRIUMPHAL MARCH FROM PETER AND THE WOLF
Serge Prokofiev (1891–1953)

Rhythmic schematic of measures 5–12:

melody

l.h. chords

bass line

There are three easily distinguishable textural elements: (1) the melodic line, which is the highest voice in the right hand or treble staff; (2) the middle-register chords found in the bass clef on beats two and four; and (3) the bass line, the lowest notes in the left-hand part occurring on beats one and three. (See the rhythmic schematic.)

The melodic line uses both dynamic accents (as in measures 5, 6, 7, 9, 10, etc.) and agogic accents (as in measures 5, 9, and 10). The rhythmic patterns within each measure clearly support the meter and are frequently repeated from measure to measure.

As we would expect, the beat is clearly established in the bass line and the accompanimental left-hand chords, the bass line having the accented beats with the chords coming on the weak beats.

Waltzes and most other **genres** (types of compositions) having origins in dance music establish the meter in ways similar to the Prokofiev march. The bass line here marks the downbeat, and the chords come on the upbeats. The melody uses agogics and patterns that support the meter. Note again the repetitions and consequent limited variety of rhythms.

WALTZ IN B-FLAT MAJOR
Franz Schubert (1797–1828)

In the following instance, the bass marks the beat and the chords come "off the beat":

THE THUNDERER MARCH
John Philip Sousa (1854–1932)

The melodic pattern of the bass notes themselves establishes the strong-weak differentiation.

There are many variations of this scheme. Here are two additional examples:

MARCH MILITAIRE
Franz Schubert (1797–1828)

THE STARS AND STRIPES FOREVER (TRIO)
John Philip Sousa (1854–1932)

Melodic rhythms are more subtle, but can also establish a metric pattern. Consider the following examples:

PRELUDE
Johann Sebastian Bach (1685–1750)

SONATA, OP. 2, NO. 1, THIRD MOVEMENT
Ludwig Beethoven (1770–1827)

WRITTEN
EXERCISES

Listen to the following examples and then write out and analyze the rhythms of both melody and accompaniment. What is the beat unit? Where is the beat most clearly established—melody or accompaniment? In which voice? Is the meter simple or compound? What characteristic rhythmic patterns occur? How are accented beats, particularly downbeats, established?

EXAMPLE 1.   "TOREADOR SONG" FROM *CARMEN*
Georges Bizet (1838–1875)

EXAMPLE 2.   "BOIL THAT CABBAGE DOWN"
Traditional

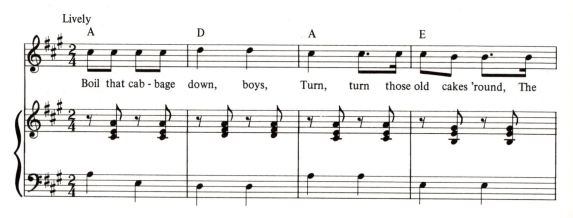

Boil that cab - bage down,   boys,   Turn,   turn those old   cakes 'round,   The

on - ly song I ev-er did sing was Boil that cab - bage down.___

EXAMPLE 3. "KNIGHT RUPERT"
Robert Schumann (1810 – 1856)

EXAMPLE 4.   "VENETIAN BOAT SONG"
Felix Mendelssohn (1809–1847)

EXAMPLE 5.   ALLEGRO IN F
Franz Josef Haydn (1732–1809)

EXAMPLE 6. "OH, WHAT A BEAUTIFUL MORNIN'"
Richard Rodgers (1902–1980)

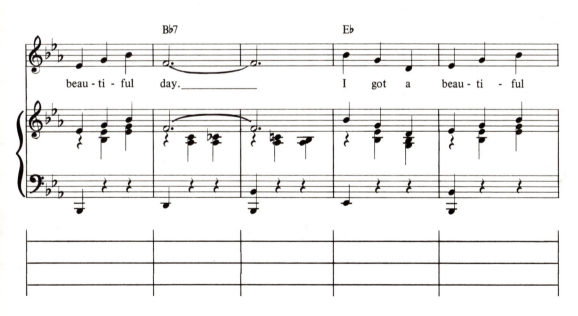

Reprinted by permission of Hal Leonard Publishing Corporation.

SYNCOPATION

Listen and then write out the rhythms to this famous Scott Joplin rag:

"THE EASY WINNERS"
Scott Joplin (1868–1917)

Notice how many instances there are of longer notes coming on weak beats and weak parts of beats. Agogic or dynamic accents that disagree with the meter are called **syncopations.** Syncopations are used for variety, but will only be effective if the metric organization is clearly established. Typically, a composer will start with regular rhythms and then use syncopations for effect. Or, as in the Joplin rag, syncopated melodic rhythms are used against regular accompanimental rhythms. Here are other examples.

EXAMPLE 1.   MARCH IN D MAJOR
Johann Sebastian Bach (1685–1750)

EXAMPLE 2.   ITALIAN FOLKSONG
Peter Tchaikovsky (1840–1893)

sempre staccato

EXAMPLE 3.   "I Got Rhythm"
George Gershwin (1898–1937)

EXAMPLE 4. "HEY JUDE"
John Lennon (1940–1980) and Paul McCartney (1942–   )

Hey Jude,____ don't make it bad, take a sad song__ and make it bet-ter.__ Re-

mem-ber to let her in - to your heart, then you can start____ to make it_ bet - ter.__

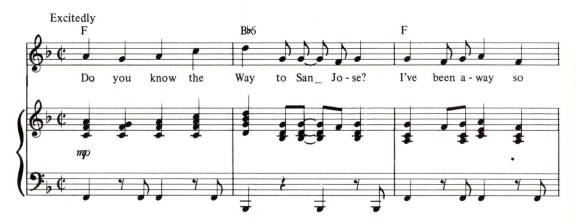

EXAMPLE 5. "DO YOU KNOW THE WAY TO SAN JOSE?"
Burt Bacharach (1929–   )

Do you know the Way to San_ Jo - se? I've been a-way so

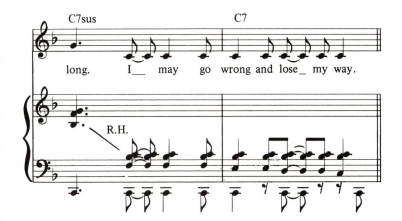

Another typical Bacharach example appears on page 76.
Syncopation can also be effected by dynamic accents:

SYMPHONY NO. 104, THIRD MOVEMENT
Franz Josef Haydn (1732–1809)

And syncopation can even result from melodic patterning:

"MÊLONS! COUPONS!" FROM *CARMEN*
Georges Bizet (1838–1875)

One very effective and common device for creating syncopation through patterning is to devise a musical motive or figure having an odd number of notes, or a number that doesn't coincide with the normal organization of the meter. The rhythmic pattern is then "superimposed" on the regular meter, creating a rhythmic disjunction or rhythmic "dissonance." Here are some examples:

"FASCINATIN' RHYTHM"
George Gershwin (1898–1937)

"IN THE MOOD"
Joe Garland (1903–   )

This device is sometimes called **isorhythm**, from the root *iso*, meaning "the same."

Here is an example that combines agogic and dynamic accents along with an isorhythmic pattern in the accompaniment:

"WALK ON BY"
Burt Bacharach (1929–   )

Copyright Blue Seas Music, Inc. and Jac Music Co., Inc. Used by permission.

Isorhythmic patterns are often notated with irregular beaming. Since the first of any beamed group suggests an accent, syncopations are created by beaming "against" the meter.

This is why it is important not to beam randomly!

CHAPTER 2   RHYTHM AND METER
   3.   PLAYING PRACTICE—SIMPLE METERS
       LEVEL 3—SYNCOPATION
       LEVEL 4—ALL OF THE ABOVE
   6.   PLAYING PRACTICE—COMPOUND METERS
       LEVEL 3—SYNCOPATION
       LEVEL 4—ALL OF THE ABOVE

CREATIVE EXERCISES   Compose your own rhythm phrases. Start with rhythms that are metrically clear and straightforward. Some more complex rhythms or syncopations may be introduced for variety. End with a longer note on an accented beat.

Three

SOUND

SOUND HAS MANY PROPERTIES. Musical notation primarily is concerned with two: *pitch*, the relative highness or lowness of the sound; and *duration*, the length in time of the sound.

Other important properties include:

1. **Timbre,** referring to the "color" of the sound. This is the property that allows us to distinguish among the various instruments, but it may refer more generally to the brightness or dullness or darkness of a sound.
2. **Dynamics,** referring to the loudness or softness of the sound.
3. **Articulation,** referring to the manner in which the sound is initiated and concluded.

THE OVERTONE SERIES

One of the most precise ways of describing a given sound is in scientific terms. Sound is a physical phenomenon and is thus an important branch of physics research.

To the physicist, sound is produced by vibrations that are transmitted through the air from a given vibrating medium to the complex receiver that is the human ear. The vibrating medium might be the string of a guitar or violin, or a column of air as in a trumpet, or a solid body as with certain percussion instruments.

These vibrations can be measured and analyzed. The number of vibrations that occur in a second gives us the **frequency.** Frequency is calculated in cycles per second or hertz (abbreviated Hz.). The fewer the hertz, the lower the pitch. The lowest audible sound is somewhere around 15 Hz., the highest 15,000 (15K) Hz. The low A on the piano is 27.5 Hz., and the highest C is 4186 Hz.

Almost all vibrations in nature consist of a complex of vibrations at various frequencies that are mathematically related. The lowest of this complex of **partials** is called the **fundamental** and it is the primary determinant of the pitch of the sound. The strength or **amplitude** of the higher partials (called **overtones** or **harmonics**) determines the timbre of the sound. The whole series of overtones can be graphically represented by a series of pitches called the **overtone series.** Here are the first 12 members of the series on C:

The first overtone (second partial) is of some importance. The ratio of vibration of overtone to fundamental is $2:1$. This is the closest possible relationship except $1:1$ and makes these two pitches sound in a sense identical, except for register. These two pitches have the same letter-name, as we have seen, and form the interval of the **octave,** a term essentially describing the musical distance between the two pitches. The octave, as we will see, becomes the basic "framing" interval for scales.

DYNAMICS

Loudness and softness are indicated in music by **dynamic markings.** These are abbreviations of the original Italian terms:

1. *p* is short for *piano* and means soft.
2. *f* is short for *forte* and means loud.
3. *m* is short for *mezzo* and is a qualifier meaning moderately. In combination, *mp* means somewhat soft and *mf* means somewhat loud.
4. *pp* stands for *pianissimo* and means very soft.
5. *ff* stands for *fortissimo* and means very loud.

Other degrees can be indicated by stringing out additional *p*'s and *f*'s: *ppp, pppp, fff,* etc.

Dynamic changes can be indicated two ways:

1.  or *crescendo* (*cresc.*) means to increase the volume.
2. ▷ or *diminuendo* (*dim.*) means to decrease the volume.

ARTICULATIONS

There are a number of symbols that you will encounter in a piece of music that tell the performer how to attack or release the sound:

1. **Slurs.** Notes falling within the curved lined are played or sung in a very **legato** (connected) manner.

The slur should not be confused with the tie, which can only connect the same pitches:

2. **Tenuto marks** indicate holding out the note full value: ♩. A series of tenuto notes would also be very legato.

3. **Staccato dots** indicate a light, clean attack and may mean that the notes are to be slightly shortened or separated.

A dot at the end of a slur indicates a lifting or shortening of the last note.

4. Accent marks are attack intensifiers and imply a certain additional volume or intensity. The most common ones are >, ∧, ∧̣, and ▾.

Closely related are the symbols *sfz* and *sf*, which stand for *sforzando*, and are used to indicate a strong accent. Accent marks generally imply separation or *non-legato*.

MUSIC FOR STUDY   Look at the following musical examples. Interpret the dynamic and articulation marks in each.

EXAMPLE 1.   "MEMORIES OF THE OPERA"
Robert Schumann (1810–1856)

EXAMPLE 2.   THE WASHINGTON POST MARCH (TRIO)
John Philip Sousa (1854–1932)

EXAMPLE 3.   "HUNTING SONG"
              Robert Schumann (1810–1856)

CHAPTER 8   LOOKING AT MUSIC
   1.   MUSICAL TERMS—LEVEL 1—DYNAMIC INDICATIONS

Four

SCALES

HALF STEPS AND WHOLE STEPS

We earlier cited the importance of the octave, with its unique acoustical "sameness" and its consequent structural significance in defining a given register and providing the "boundary" or framing interval for scales.

Theoretically, we could divide the octave into any number of smaller intervals. The scientist uses a standard division into 100 increments (called **cents**) for purposes of making fine distinctions in the size or **tuning** of musical intervals. Musicians are very concerned about good **intonation,** or playing in tune. This refers to the ability to match pitches and to play pitches neither sharp (too high) nor flat (too low). For practical reasons, music uses a much smaller number of intervals. The usual number is 12 equal increments, though some folk music and contemporary music uses up to 24.

To see this standard division, it helps to look at a piano keyboard. We notice a pattern of seven white and five black keys that repeats in each octave or register.

The smallest increment is represented by adjacent keys, either white to black or, in two cases, white to white. This interval is called a **semitone** or **half step.** By skipping a key, we find the interval of a **tone** or **whole step.** Most scales are basically composed of whole steps and half steps.

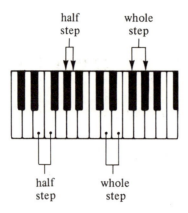

 CHAPTER 4   SCALES

WHOLE STEPS AND HALF STEPS

1. WHOLE & HALF STEPS ON THE KEYBOARD

Up to this point, we have identified only the pitches represented by the white keys on the piano. Even though there are only five black keys, they give us a total of ten additional pitches. Each black key can represent both a raising of one white key pitch or a lowering of another. If we move to the right from a white key (say C) to the immediately adjacent black key, we say we have raised the pitch a half step. We place a symbol, called a **sharp,** in front of the note and call the new note C sharp (C♯).

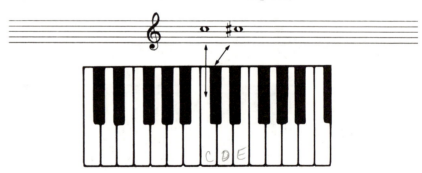

Similarly, if we move to the left (say from E), we say we have lowered the pitch a half step. We place a symbol, called a **flat,** in front of the note and call the new note E flat (E♭).

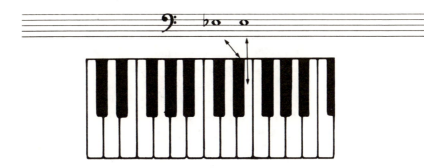

Curiously, even though the sharp or flat goes in front of the note in the music itself, we say it *after* the letter, as in A *flat* or G *sharp*. There is a common tendency at first to get mixed up and put the sharp or flat after the note in the music:

Check yourself. The sharp or flat always goes in front of the note.

We can now identify all notes of the keyboard, noting that each black key normally represents *two* pitches.

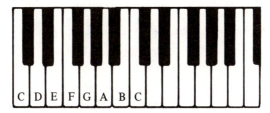

CHAPTER 4   SCALES

WHOLE STEPS AND HALF STEPS
   2.   WHOLE & HALF STEP RECOGNITION
   3.   WHOLE & HALF STEP SPELLING

There are actually five symbols that we use to represent raised or lowered pitches. These symbols are called **accidentals.** In addition to the sharp and flat, we have the **natural sign** (♮), which cancels another accidental; the

double sharp (×), which raises a sharped note another half step; and the **double flat** (♭♭), which lowers a flatted note another half step.

Accidentals can be applied to any note. If we take the note B and sharp it we have B sharp (B♯). This note is played on the key we normally call C, since the adjacent key to B is another white key. Pitches that are named differently but are played on the same key on the piano are called **enharmonic.** Other examples would be F♯ and G♭, E♭ and D♯, E♮ and F♭, and so on.

It follows that any letter-name could have five different pitches associated with it. Illustrated with G's, they are:

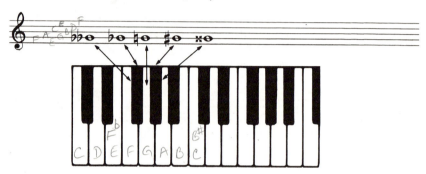

This gives us many more pitches than would appear from just looking at the keyboard, and there are uses for all of them. The apparent discrepancy between the number of named pitches and the number of keys on the piano is accounted for by those enharmonics. We will see that there is a big difference between, say, F♯ and G♭, and on certain instruments the two pitches even have slightly different frequencies and thus pitches. We call these discrepancies **tuning differentials,** and the way the note is written or tuned depends entirely on the context in which that note occurs.

We can also see now that there are two ways of notating a half step on the keyboard: by using the same letter-name, for example C to C♯; by using the adjacent letter-name, for example C to D♭. (These half steps are themselves enharmonic, as we will see when we discuss intervals in Chapter 5.) The half step involving two letter-names is called a **diatonic half step** and is the form found in almost all scales. That with the same letter-name is called a **chromatic half step,** and is found only in the chromatic scale. Which we choose is based on the context of the music.

We should point out here that whole steps must always be spelled with *adjacent* letter names. E♮ to F♯ is a whole step, but E♮ to G♭, even though played on the same keys of the piano, is not.

CHAPTER 4   SCALES
WHOLE STEPS AND HALF STEPS
    4. ENHARMONICS

WRITTEN
EXERCISES

Once you feel you have mastered the computer exercises presented so far in this chapter, do the following:

1.   Write the note one whole step *above* the given note.

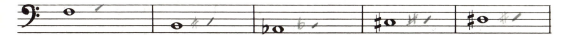

2.   Write the note one whole step *below* the given note.

3.   Write the note that is a *diatonic* half step *above*.

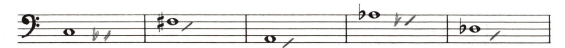

4.   Write the note that is a *diatonic* half step *below*.

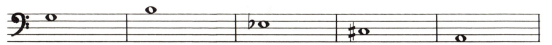

5. Write the note that is a *chromatic* half step *above*.

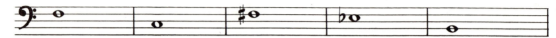

6. Write the note that is a *chromatic* half step *below*.

7. Write a note that is *enharmonic* to the given note.

THE MAJOR SCALE

Here is the music to the familiar tune "Home, Sweet Home."

"HOME, SWEET HOME"
Sir Henry Bishop (1786–1855)

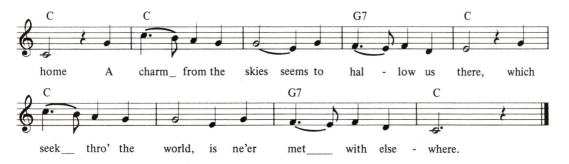

home   A   charm_ from the   skies   seems to   hal - low   us   there,   which

seek__ thro' the   world,   is   ne'er   met____ with   else - where.

At first glance, there is much diversity in the music—the total number of pitches, the direction of the line, the various rhythms, and so on. But a closer examination reveals that there are actually only seven different pitches in this piece. It should also be apparent that the composer was very selective in the order and arrangement of those pitches. We sense a plan or a design, and we feel a certain satisfaction or completeness when the song is over.

The techniques whereby the composer organizes the raw pitch material comprise one of the most important areas of musical study.

In the example above, notice particularly the importance of the note C. Not only is it the first pitch and the last pitch, but it is the highest pitch and the lowest pitch. Thus it acts somewhat as a frame, or point of reference, for the piece. This pitch is called the **key note,** or **tonic,** and the music is said to be *in the key* of that note. The way in which the other pitches relate to C can be more easily studied if we arrange the pitches in ascending order, starting on C.

For convenience, we number the pitches, or **scale degrees,** from lowest to highest.

We now have a **scale.** A scale is defined as an arrangement of pitches in systematic, ascending order. The term comes from the Italian *scala,* which literally means ladder. There are obviously many scales, and they are differentiated by the specific placement of whole and half steps. This placement, along with all the other note-to-note relationships within the scale, accounts for the particular flavor of music based on a particular scale. We will have occasion to compare the sounds of various scales as we discuss them in turn.

Returning to the scale derived from "Home, Sweet Home," we find the following pattern of whole steps and half steps:

This pattern defines this scale as a **major scale,** and we call this particular scale a C-major scale. Any scale having the same whole step–half step arrangement will have the same sound, though at a different pitch level. We can construct a major scale on any pitch simply by using accidentals to create the necessary whole steps and half steps.

Let's build a major scale on D. If we use just the white notes of the piano, we know our half steps will fall in the wrong places.

Since we need a whole step from scale degree 2 to 3, we raise the F to F♯. This now gives us the needed half step from scale degree 3 to 4. Similarly, by raising C to C♯, we get a whole step from 6 to 7 and a half step from 7 to 8.

Compare the sound of this scale to that of the C-major scale. The D-major scale will sound identical, only a whole step higher.

Let's build a major scale on F. With the white notes, we have a whole step from 3 to 4.

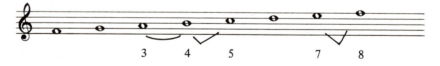

We must make this a half step by *lowering* B to B♭. We now have an F-major scale.

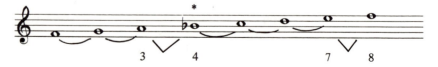

Note that the half steps must always be diatonic half steps, that is, using adjacent scale degrees, as in A to B♭. A to A♯ would be incorrect, and would in fact result in the omission of a scale degree!

We can start on raised or lowered notes as well.

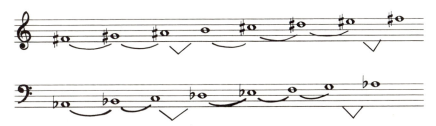

In common usage, major scales are found on all these pitches: C, C♯, D♭, D, E♭, E, F, F♯, G♭, G, A♭, A, B♭, B, and C♭.

CHAPTER 4   SCALES

THE MAJOR SCALE

1. MAJOR SCALE WRITING—ALL LEVELS
2. MAJOR SCALE SPELLING—ALL LEVELS
3. MAJOR SCALE RECOGNITION—ALL LEVELS

WRITTEN EXERCISES

When you feel you have mastered the computer drills, work out the following written exercises. As before, these exercises are designed to develop the manual skills of actually writing music and to check your comprehension of the materials away from the computer. Your instructor may wish to have these exercises handed in for purposes of evaluation.

1. Add accidentals to make the following scales major:

2. Construct major scales on the given pitches, using accidentals as needed. Write your scales in one octave from tonic to tonic. Label whole and half steps.

KEY SIGNATURES FOR MAJOR KEYS

Look at this example of piano music written with all accidentals.

FUGUE NO. 13 FROM *THE WELL-TEMPERED CLAVIER,* BOOK I
Johann Sebastian Bach (1685–1750)

In cases where the same notes are consistently altered throughout a piece, it is far easier to use a **key signature.**

A key signature simply takes all the necessary accidentals and places them in a particular order at the beginning of every staff. The following scales illustrate this procedure:

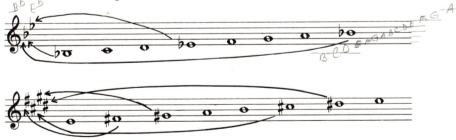

Note that one accidental in a key signature applies to every pitch having that same letter-name, regardless of register.

The order of sharps and flats in the key signature reflects the relationship of the scales and keys themselves.

If we start with a C-major scale, which has no sharps or flats, and then build a major scale starting on G, the fifth degree, we find that this scale requires one sharp.

In a like manner, if we built a scale on D, the fifth degree of G major, we find that this scale requires two sharps, and so on.

Here are the key signatures in order of increasing sharps for all major keys with sharps.

Note that in each case the last sharp in the key signature is the seventh degree of the scale, and we can always determine the key note or tonic of any major key by going up one half step from the last accidental.

Let's repeat the same process starting with the C-major scale, but instead going *down* five steps or *up* four steps. Building a major scale on F requires one flat in the signature.

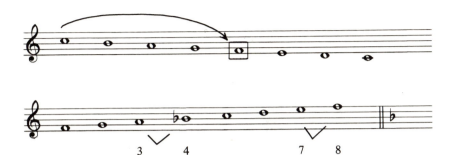

Building a major scale on B♭, five degrees down from F, requires two flats, and so on.

This procedure will give us all the major keys with flats.

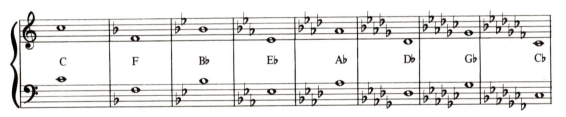

Note that in each case the last flat in the signature is for the *fourth* scale degree. To find tonic, merely count down four letter-names; alternatively, with key signatures having more than one flat, the letter-name of the next-to-the-last flat will be tonic.

Note that the letter order of the flat keys is the reverse of the letter order of the sharp keys, and that the letter order of the flats themselves—B E A D G C F—is the reverse of the letter order of the sharps—F C G D A E B.

This ordering of keys five steps apart is often called the **circle of fifths** and is graphically illustrated as follows:

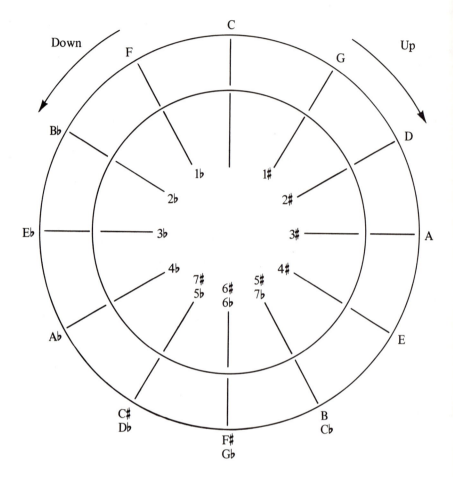

Although theoretically a spiral, the circle is "closed" with those keys that are enharmonic: C♯ and D♭, F♯ and G♭, and B and C♭.

CHAPTER 4   SCALES

THE MAJOR SCALE

    4.   MAJOR KEY SIGNATURE SPELLING—ALL LEVELS

    5.   MAJOR KEY SIGNATURE RECOGNITION—ALL LEVELS

WRITTEN
EXERCISES

When writing key signatures, check to be sure the accidentals are in the proper order and neatly and clearly placed on the correct line or space.

1. Identify the major keys designated by the following key signatures:

a. Bb MAJ   b. G MAJ   c. Ab MAJ   d. F# MAJ   e. Cb MAJ

f. D MAJ   g. Eb MAJ   h. C# MAJ   i. E MAJ   j. Db MAJ

2. Write the key signatures for the following major keys:

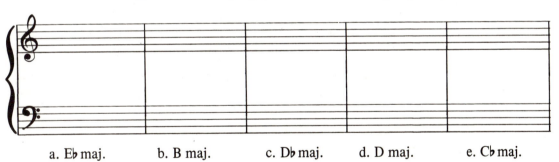

a. Eb maj.   b. B maj.   c. Db maj.   d. D maj.   e. Cb maj.

f. F maj.   g. A maj.   h. G♭ maj.   i. C maj.   j. E maj.

INTERVALS IN THE MAJOR SCALE

When we talk about music, we are talking about note *relationships*. These are manifold, and all are important—a given note may be shorter or longer than another, higher or lower, louder or softer. The notes may be close together or far apart; they may be played together or separately.

Any two notes form what we call an **interval;** intervals are really the most basic building blocks of musical structures. Intervals have two important properties: *size* and *quality*.

Size refers to the distance from one note to another in terms of scale degrees. This distance is designated by an arabic number. Whole steps and diatonic half steps are both technically *seconds*, since both intervals encompass *two* scale degrees. Seconds are symbolized by an arabic 2. The difference between the whole-step second and the half-step second is what is referred to as **quality,** and is a measurement of the semitone content of the interval. We call the whole step a *major* second, abbreviated M2, since the whole step consists of two half steps; major here means *large* second. We call the half step itself a *minor* second, abbreviated m2; minor here means *small* second. The difference between a major and minor second is, of course, a half step.

Here is a summary of the seconds found in the major scale:

M2   M2   m2   M2   M2   M2   m2

Intervals that encompass three scale degrees are called *thirds* and are symbolized by an arabic 3. Like seconds, the thirds in the major scale are either major or minor.

The third from tonic to the third scale degree in the major mode consists of two whole steps.

This third is *major*. The third from scale degrees 2 to 4, however, is only a step and a half.

This third is *minor*. And so on, up the scale:

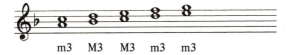

The major thirds are especially important in giving the major scale its "flavor."

In like fashion, an interval encompassing four scale degrees is a *fourth*, five degrees a *fifth*, and so on.

Intervals are an important part of the study of music, and we will devote an entire chapter to a complete and detailed treatment.

NAMES OF THE SCALE DEGREES

Music that uses predominantly the tones of a given scale and is organized around the tonic pitch is termed **tonal**, and the music is said to be in a **key.** For example, music that uses the G-major scale is said to be in the key of G major; music that uses the E♭-major scale is in the key of E♭ major.

In traditional tonal music, the tones of the scale tend to fall into recognizable and predictable patterns. Understanding the relationships among the various scale degrees is central to a broader understanding of the music itself. The names of the scale degrees give us clues to these relationships.

The first scale degree is the **tonic** and is the pitch toward which all the other pitches gravitate.

The fifth scale degree is called the **dominant.** It is second in importance to the tonic and tends to be a very important structural pitch, along with tonic.

The third scale degree is the **mediant,** so called because it lies halfway between tonic and dominant. These three pitches together outline the **tonic triad.** (Triads will be fully explained in Chapter 6.)

1   3   5   tonic triad

The second scale degree is called the **supertonic,** because it lies one step above the tonic. It frequently acts as a neighbor to the tonic or is used in passing from tonic to mediant.

The fourth scale degree is called the **subdominant,** because it lies five steps *below* the tonic. The subdominant also lies a half step above the mediant and has a strong tendency to move toward it. It may also be used in passing from mediant to dominant.

The sixth scale degree is called the **submediant,** as it lies halfway between the tonic and subdominant. The submediant frequently acts as a neighbor to the dominant, or in passing from dominant to the upper tonic.

The seventh scale degree is called the **leading tone,** as it tends to lead into the tonic. This tendency is established by the half step between the two scale degrees.

MUSIC FOR STUDY
You will recall from our earlier example of "Home, Sweet Home" that melodies move in a variety of ways. At times, the melody moves by step from scale degree to scale degree. This motion is called **scalar** or **conjunct.** At other times, the melody skips from one scale degree to another. This is called **disjunct** motion. In addition, pitches may be directly repeated. Melodies typically use all three types of motion.

Any scale is, strictly speaking, an abstraction. It represents a systematic arrangement of the pitch material that has been used in a piece of music. Much of the time, melodies use only fragments of scales, moving in either direction, but there are instances where complete scales appear. These melodies let us see, in a preliminary way, the way the music is organized, and the parts that the various scale degrees play.

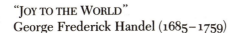

"JOY TO THE WORLD"
George Frederick Handel (1685–1759)

What is the key of this piece? Note all the occurrences of the tonic. Next, note the occurrences of dominant and mediant. Finally, consider how the other scale degrees are used in relationship to tonic, dominant, and mediant. Note particularly where the half steps of the scale occur.

Some of the factors that influence how we hear these relationships are:

1. Metric placement—notes that fall on accented beats are generally felt to be structurally more significant.

2. Longer notes are also felt to be more important.

3. Pitches that *initiate* musical motions are often important, and certainly those pitches that *conclude* musical motions are important.

Here is another familiar Christmas carol:

"THE FIRST NOEL"
Traditional

cer - tain poor Shep-herds in fields as they lay. In___ fields___ where

they lay_ keep-ing their sheep On a cold win-ter's night__ that

was__ so deep. No - el___ No - el, No - el, No - el,

Born is the king__ of Is - ra - el.

Again, notice how the melody is "anchored" by the tonic and dominant, with the mediant as a third point of reference.

Here are several other examples of predominantly scalar music.

EXAMPLE 1.   PIANO TRIO, OP. 97
Ludwig Beethoven (1770–1827)

EXAMPLE 2.   "CARO NOME" FROM *RIGOLETTO*
Giuseppe Verdi (1813–1901)

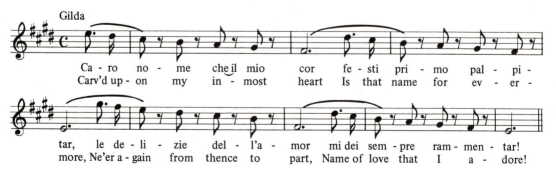

Ca - ro no - me che il mio cor fe - sti pri - mo pal - pi -
Carv'd up - on my in - most heart Is that name for ev - er -

tar, le de - li - zie del - l'a - mor mi dei sem - pre ram - men - tar!
more, Ne'er a - gain from thence to part, Name of love that I a - dore!

EXAMPLE 3.   "THE EASY WINNERS"
Scott Joplin (1868–1917)

EXAMPLE 4.   "EVERYBODY'S GOT A HOME BUT ME"
Richard Rodgers (1902–1980)
Lyrics by Oscar Hammerstein II (1895–1960)

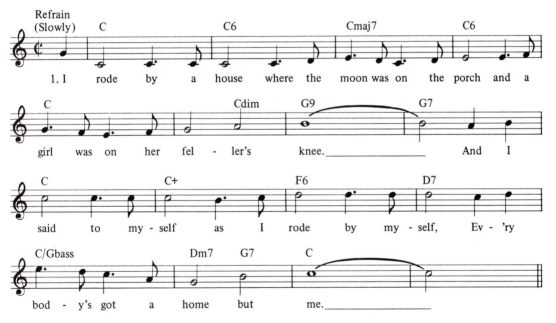

Reprinted by permission of Hal Leonard Publishing Corporation.

Note in the following popular melody how the presence of the half steps establishes F as tonic of the scale, even though the pitch F is not heard prominently until the very end. Note also how the leap from D to E in the next-to-last measure actually completes the scale, but in a lower register.

EXAMPLE 5.   "THE SOUND OF MUSIC"
Richard Rodgers (1902–1980)
Lyrics by Oscar Hammerstein II (1895–1960)

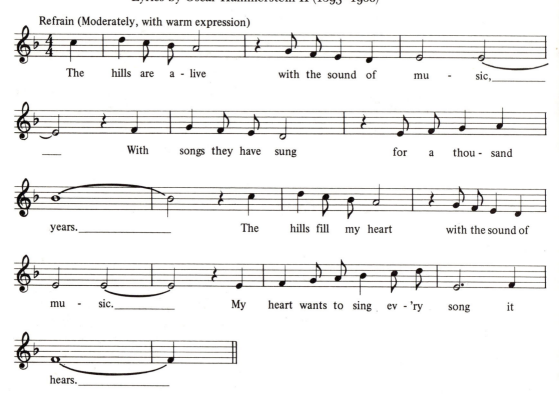

Reprinted by permission of Hal Leonard Publishing Corporation.

How do the arrival points on E in measures 3 and 11, and the arrival on B♭ in measure 7, contribute to the sense of forward motion in this melody? What is the effect of "withholding" tonic until the very end?*

From the preceding, we might draw a few conclusions. The tonic, dominant, and mediant are frequently used as points of arrival or rest, and, in fact, we often call them *inactive* scale degrees. The other pitches tend to act as passing notes or neighboring notes and we call these pitches *active* scale degrees. Like so much in music, these principles are by no means hard and fast, and we will see ample latitude in their application. Nonethe-

_____

*Harmonic considerations are obviously very important in this melody, but must await our full discussion of chords in Chapter 6.

less, this is an important concept, and one that is basic to understanding musical organization.

The Minor Mode

SUGGESTED LISTENING Franz Schubert, "Frülingssehnsucht" from *Schwanengesang*, mm. 13–30 (first verse); mm. 103–123 (third verse)

Johannes Brahms, "Vergebliches Ständchen," mm. 1–20 (first verse); mm. 43–60 (third verse)

Bedřich Smetana, *The Moldau*, mm. 40–49; mm. 333–350

Peter Tchaikovsky, Symphony No. 5, first movement, mm. 1–8; fourth movement, mm. 1–8, mm. 474–481

Cole Porter, "I Love Paris," refrain, mm. 1–16; mm. 17–36

Michel Legrand, Theme from *Summer of '42*, mm. 1–8; mm. 9–25

Discuss the difference in mood or character between the paired examples in each piece.

Aside from some obvious differences in register, dynamics, and instrumentation, all these examples illustrate the dramatic contrast of **mode.** We often associate mode changes with mood: music in the major mode seems brighter and more cheerful, maybe even optimistic. The other commonly used mode—the **minor mode**—seems darker, more somber, even sad. The term mode, strictly defined, refers to the exact placement of half steps within the seven-tone scale. There are actually a number of modes, but for the time being we will only be concerned with two of them—major and minor.

The major mode is, of course, represented by the major scale. The minor mode is a bit more problematic, since there are three forms that the scale may take.

Consider these well-known folk tunes. All have been written out in the same key (E minor) for ease of comparison.

EXAMPLE 1.   "GOD REST YE MERRY, GENTLEMEN"
Traditional

EXAMPLE 2.   "QUE NE SUIS-JE LA FOUGÈRE"
Traditional French

EXAMPLE 3.   "GREENSLEEVES"
Traditional

We notice that the first five notes of each scale are uniform and have the pattern whole–half–whole–whole:

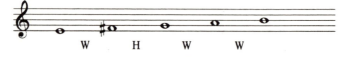

CHAPTER 4   SCALES
MINOR MODE
　　1.   MINOR SCALE WRITING—ALL LEVELS
　　2.   MINOR SCALE SPELLING—ALL LEVELS
　　3.   MINOR SCALE RECOGNITION

WRITTEN   As before, when you feel you have mastered the computer drills, work out
EXERCISES   the following written exercises. Your instructor may wish to have these
exercises handed in for purposes of evaluation.

　　1.   Add accidentals as required to make the following scales *natural
minor:*

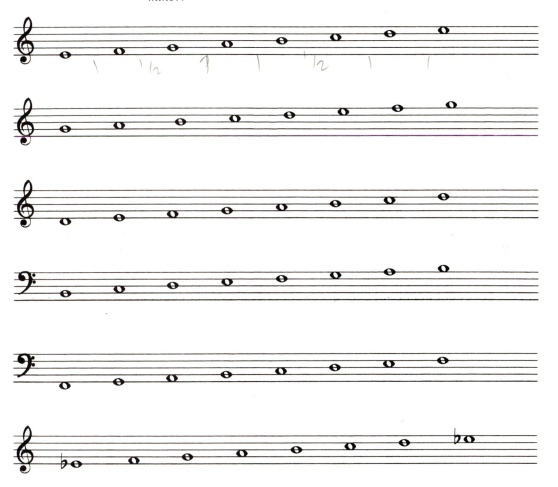

2. Make the following minor scales *harmonic* by adding the necessary accidental:

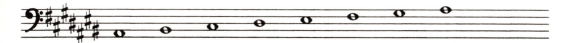

3. Make the following minor scales *melodic* by adding the necessary accidentals:

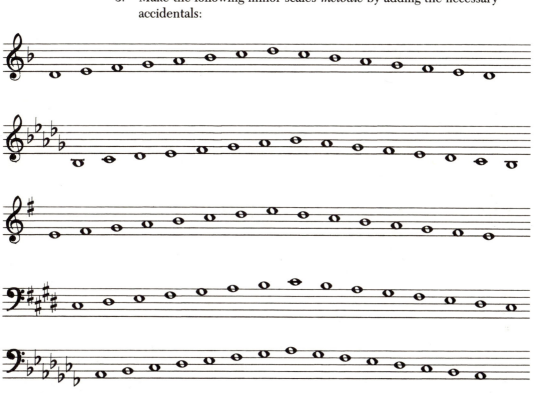

INTERVALS IN THE MINOR MODE

Here are the seconds and thirds found in the various minor scales. Compare them with those found in the major scale. It is the difference in these intervals that gives the minor mode *its* unique "flavor."

| M2 | m2 | M2 | M2 | m2 | M2 | M2 | A2 | M2 | M2 | m2 |

RELATIVE AND PARALLEL MINORS

Every major key has both a relative and a parallel minor. (This relationship works both ways, of course. Every minor key has both a relative and parallel major.)

If we start on the sixth scale degree of any major scale and build a complete scale, we arrive at a natural minor scale. It follows that any major and its **relative minor** will share the same pitches and consequently the same key signature.

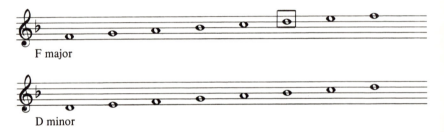

F major

D minor

The corollary of this is that every key signature will represent both a major key and a minor key. We can now illustrate the circle of fifths with both modes for each key signature. Note: On this chart, and elsewhere in this book, capital letters represent major keys, while lowercase letters represent minor keys.

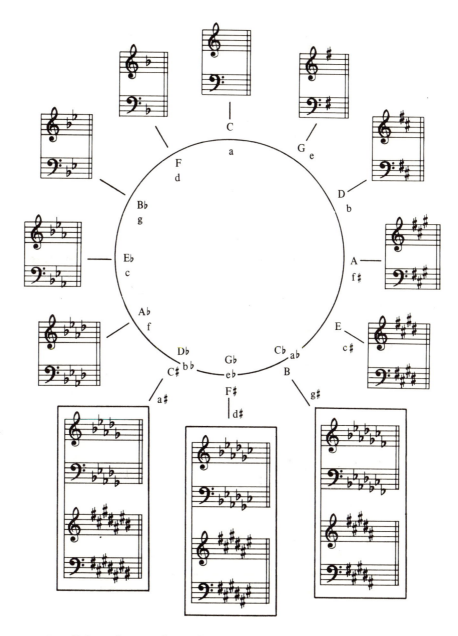

Parallel modes are those that share the same tonic. Examples are C major and C minor, A major and A minor, E♭ major and E♭ minor, etc. Parallel modes obviously have different key signatures, and, in fact, there is a consistent difference of three accidentals between parallel modes.

F: f: E: e: D: d:

A comparison of parallel modes indicates certain common pitches. We often call the tonic, dominant, and subdominant **tonal degrees,** since they are the same in parallel modes. The other scale degrees are called **modal degrees,** since they vary from mode to mode. Of particular importance are the mediant and the submediant. What common pitches or pitch patterns exist among the various scale forms?

CHAPTER 4   SCALES

MINOR MODE
    4.   MINOR KEY SIGNATURE SPELLING—ALL LEVELS
    5.   MINOR KEY SIGNATURE RECOGNITION—ALL LEVELS
    6.   KEY SIGNATURE RECOGNITION (MAJOR AND MINOR)—ALL LEVELS

WRITTEN
EXERCISES

1.   Name the *relative* key of each given key. Write out the key signatures and tonics of both keys, using both clefs of the great staff.
    Example: Given key: F major   Relative: D minor

Given key   Relative

a.   D major

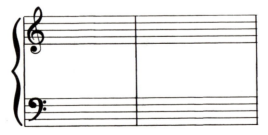

b.   C minor

c.   A♭ major

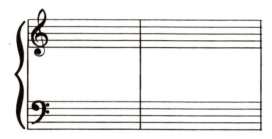

d.   F♯ minor

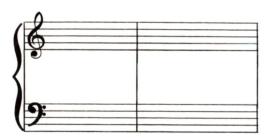

e.   G major

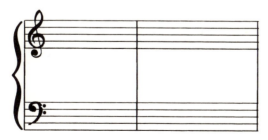

2. Name the *parallel* key of each given key. Write out the key signature
    and tonic note of both keys, using both clefs of the great staff.
    Example: Given key: G major   Parallel: G minor

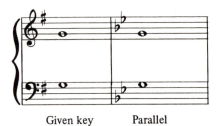

    Given key   Parallel

    a.   B♭ major

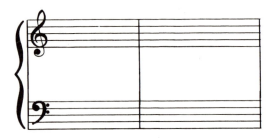

    b.   E♭ minor

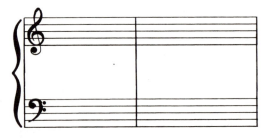

    c.   A major

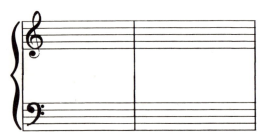

d.   C♯ major

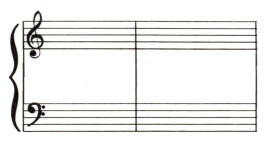

e.   B minor

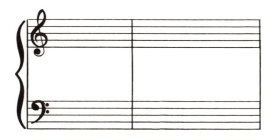

MUSIC FOR
STUDY

Look and listen to the following examples. Which note seems to be the tonic? Is the music in major or minor? What scale degrees seem most clearly to establish the mode?

EXAMPLE 1.   "O CHARLIE IS MY DARLING"
Scotch Song

Char- lie is my dar - ling, my dar - ling, my dar - ling, O Char -lie is my dar - ling, The

young Chev - a - lier.

EXAMPLE 2.   TRIO IN G MAJOR
Franz Josef Haydn (1732–1809)

EXAMPLE 3.   SYMPHONY NO. 4, SECOND MOVEMENT
Peter Tchaikovsky (1840–1893)

EXAMPLE 4.   "FIRST LOSS"
                Robert Schumann (1810–1856)

Andante con moto

EXAMPLE 5.   "ECOSSAISE"
                Franz Schubert (1797–1828)

Allegro

EXAMPLE 6.   HUNGARIAN DANCE NO. 5
                Johannes Brahms (1833–1897)

Allegro

EXAMPLE 7. "I WONDER AS I WANDER"
Appalachian Carol

EXAMPLE 8. LOVE THEME FROM *THE GODFATHER*
Nino Rota (1911–1974)

EXAMPLE 9. "DANUBE WAVES"
Ion Ivanovici (1845–1902)

One can't always rely on the key signature (or lack of one) alone when determining the key and mode of a piece. Consider this melody by Haydn:

What is the tonic pitch of this melody? How is that pitch established as tonic? What scale degree is being raised by the sharp? What then is the scale being used?

Very often, a key signature will indicate only the overall key of an extended piece. The composer may change keys during the course of the movement and indicate the new key with accidentals only. Regardless, remember that we are only aware of the key signature itself when we are *looking* at the music, and not when we are *listening* to it. But we certainly *do* hear tonic and the particular scale being used, and it's this that tells us what key and mode we are in!

In summary, look for tonic and dominant to be established by position and frequency—at the beginning or at the end of the music, or on metric accents. In minor, look for the presence of accidentals on the seventh, and also on the sixth, scale degrees. Remember that these scale degrees are variable.

OTHER SCALES

There are a number of other scales that should be mentioned, since they are used in the music of the Middle Ages (c. 1200–1450) and the Renaissance (c. 1450–1600), and also occur in folk music and contemporary music.

The modes, sometimes called the **church modes,** are actually very old. They form the basis for most music composed prior to 1600 and have been "stored away," so to speak, in the chants of the Roman Catholic Church. The modes enjoyed a resurgence of interest in the early part of this century and appear even in popular music and jazz.

We mentioned the use of the word *mode* in regard to the location of the half steps. In this sense, the modes are merely a series of scales having slightly different arrangements of whole and half steps. We can easily visualize this by thinking of the white keys of the piano. If we start on each pitch in turn we get all the modes.

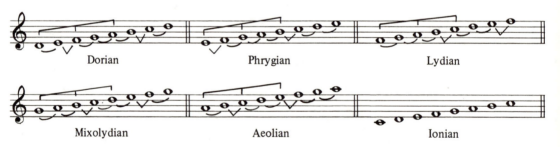

The Ionian mode is the same as C major, of course, so is often not counted as a mode. Aeolian is our now-familiar natural minor.

Any mode can be written on any pitch, of course, simply by using accidentals or the appropriate key signature. Here are examples of modes transposed to other pitches:

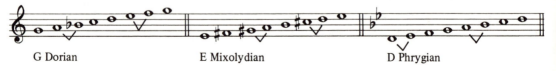

The modes are named after provinces of ancient Greece. This is handy nomenclature, but has no other significance. Dorian, Phrygian, and Aeolian are called minor modes because of the minor third (step-and-a-half) from tonic to mediant. Lydian, Mixolydian, and Ionian are major modes because of the major third (two steps) between tonic and mediant.

Modal music is *centric*, meaning that the tonic (or *final*) of the mode acts as a key center, just as in major and minor.

Here are some examples of modal music. Note how the characteristic intervals of whole step–half step patterns are emphasized. Identify the mode of each example.

EXAMPLE 1.   "SCARBOROUGH FAIR"
Traditional

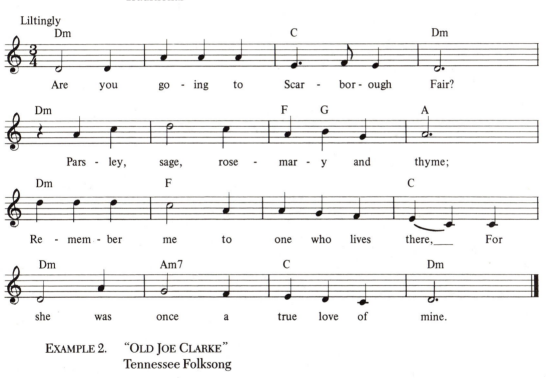

EXAMPLE 2.   "OLD JOE CLARKE"
Tennessee Folksong

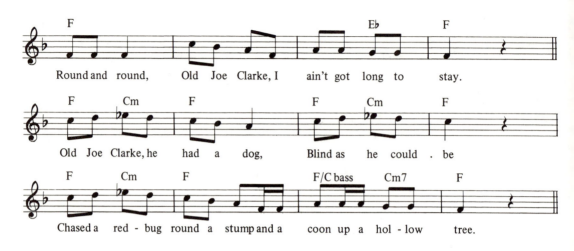

Round and round, Old Joe Clarke, I ain't got long to stay.

Old Joe Clarke, he had a dog, Blind as he could . be

Chased a red - bug round a stump and a coon up a hol - low tree.

EXAMPLE 3. "TOCCATINA"
Dmitri Kabalevsky (1904–   )

EXAMPLE 4. THEME FROM *HAWAII FIVE-O*
Mort Stevens (1929–   )

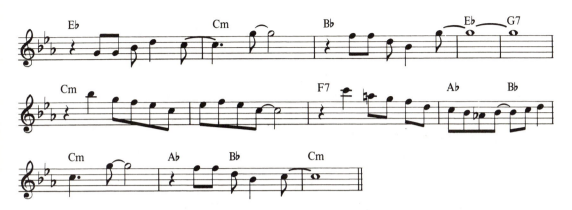

"Hawaii Five-O" words and music by Mort Stevens. © 1969 CBS, Inc. Publishing rights vested in April Music, Inc. I-M-A.

The use of A♮ in measure 12 has the effect of momentarily changing the mode. What is the mode in that measure? The appearance of A♭ in the following measure restores the original mode. This is another very common device in modal music.

SUGGESTED LISTENING

Contemporary composers of popular music have frequently used the modes to good effect. But rather than writing whole tunes in a single mode, these composers mix modes, going back and forth from the modes to conventional major and minor.

The Beatles were a rock group that enjoyed a phenomenal success during the '60s. Much of their music has a modal flavor, derived in part from their common British folk-music tradition, and from '50s American rock and roll (Bill Haley, Elvis Presley, *et al.*).

The use of the "blues" flatted seventh degree in the major mode yields the Mixolydian mode. Listen, for example, to "A Hard Day's Night" or "Ticket to Ride." "A Hard Day's Night" also has an interesting mixing of major and minor.

"Norwegian Wood" illustrates the use of contrasting modes. The first four measures are in G Mixolydian (by virtue of the lowered seventh degree), while the second four measures are in G Dorian (characterized by the progression from the G minor chord to the C major chord, which implies a G Dorian scale). The last four measures return to Mixolydian. The use of the F♯ suggests a momentary traditional G major.

"Can't Buy Me Love" is largely in Aeolian. The lovely "Eleanor Rigby" achieves its haunting effect through a mixture of Dorian and Aeolian. This is very sophisticated music!

The opening phrase of "Walk On By," by Burt Bacharach and Hal David, has a pronounced Dorian flavor:

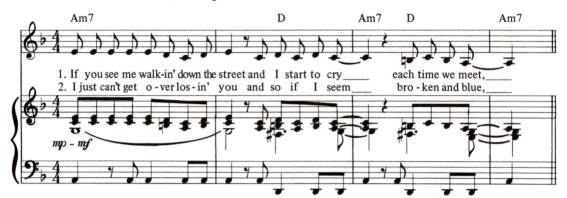

1. If you see me walk-in' down the street and I start to cry_____ each time we meet,_____
2. I just can't get o-ver los-in' you and so if I seem___ bro-ken and blue,_____

As the key signature suggests, the music progresses ultimately toward F major. You will find the last part of the tune on page 76.

The use of the raised fourth degree in major gives the melody the piquancy of the Lydian mode. Richard Rodgers uses this device in the opening phrase of "March of the Siamese Children," perhaps to suggest the exotic atmosphere of the East.

The Lydian mode also colors two of the most popular songs from Leonard Bernstein's *West Side Story*, "Maria" and "Tonight."

Still another scale is the pentatonic scale, which, as the name suggests, is a five-note scale. We know it most commonly as the scale formed by the black keys on the piano (in fact a lot of pentatonic music uses only the black keys), and we tend (incorrectly) to associate it with oriental music. Like the modes, pentatonic scales can be written on any pitch. Here is the black-key scale and two other examples:

Pentatonic music is centric and generally very simple. Much folk music is pentatonic. Here are some examples:

EXAMPLE 1.   "OLD PAINT"
            Traditional

Good - by,   old   Paint,   I'm a - leav - in' Chey - enne,   Good - by,   old

Paint,   I'm a - leav - in' Chey - enne.   I'm   leav - in' Chey - enne,   I'm   off   to Mon-

Scale:

tan - a,   Good - by,   old   Paint,   I'm a - leav - in' Chey - enne.

EXAMPLE 2.   "HUSH, MY BABE"
            Traditional American

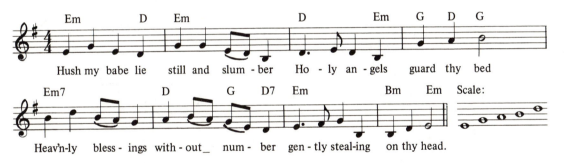

Hush my babe lie   still and   slum - ber   Ho - ly an - gels   guard thy bed

Heav'n-ly   bless - ings with - out_   num - ber   gen - tly steal-ing   on thy head.

EXAMPLE 3.   "PAGODES"
            Claude Debussy (1862–1918)

Modérément animé

p

Scale:

Composers often use unusual scales for some specific effect. These often consist of a regular pattern of intervals.

One unique scale is the aptly named **whole-tone scale.** Music using this scale will seem lacking in a secure key center and will sound either restless or have a sense of suspended motion.

WHOLE-TONE SCALE

EXAMPLE 1.   INTERLUDE FROM *MADAMA BUTTERFLY*
Giacomo Puccini (1858–1924)

The following example uses two scale forms:

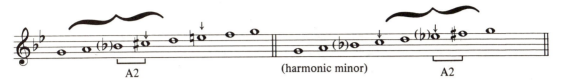

A2   (harmonic minor)   A2

Note the symmetrical pattern of steps formed by the variable fourth and sixth scale degrees.

EXAMPLE 2.   *ORIENTALE*
Cesar Cui (1835–1918)

Tradition is sometimes hard to escape. Since Cui was writing in a period where the major–minor system was dominant, he felt compelled perhaps to use the key signature for G minor, even though his scale materials were not traditional. He is thus forced to treat scale degree four as a variable along with six and seven. Might a better solution have been to use only one flat (that for the third scale degree)?

EXAMPLE 3.   "FIDDLER ON THE ROOF"
Jerry Bock (1928–   )

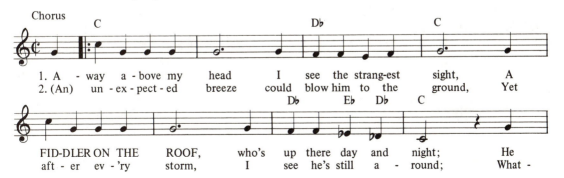

1. A - way a - bove my head   I see the strang-est sight,   A
2. (An) un - ex - pect - ed breeze could blow him to the ground,   Yet

FID-DLER ON THE ROOF,   who's up there day and night;   He
aft - er ev - 'ry storm,   I see he's still a - round;   What -

fid - dles when it   rains,   He   fid - dles when it   snows,   I've
ev - er each day   brings   This   odd out -land -ish   man;   He

nev - er   seen him   rest,   Yet   on and   on   he   goes.
plays his   sim - ple   tune,   As   sweet-ly   as   he   can.

What does   it mean, this   FID - DLER ON   THE ROOF, Who   fid - dles ev - 'ry night and

fid - dles ev - 'ry   noon?   Why should he pick   so   cu - ri - ous   a   place to

play   his   lit - tle   fid - dler's   tune?   2. An   tune?   A

FID - DLER ON   THE   ROOF,   A   most   un - like - ly   sight,   It

might not   mean   a   thing,   But   then   a - gain   it   might!

Reprinted by permission of Hal Leonard Publishing Corporation.

CHAPTER 4   SCALES

MINOR MODE

3.   **MINOR SCALE RECOGNITION—NOTICE AND LISTEN TO THE SCALES
THAT ARE *NOT* MAJOR OR MINOR.**

None of the scales discussed heretofore has consisted of more than seven different tones. It is quite possible (and quite common) to compose simple pieces using only the notes of a given scale. We term such music **diatonic.**

Yet we know from our discussion of the keyboard and accidentals that other notes are also available. These other pitches are commonly introduced as decorative pitches or for "color," and, in fact, are called **chromatic** pitches, from the Greek word *chromos,* which means color.

The most frequent embellishments using chromatically altered pitches are neighbor tones and passing tones. Here are some examples:

Chromatic passing tones are naturally used to fill in the "space" between two notes a whole step apart. If we take a major or minor scale and fill in *all* the whole steps with chromatic half steps, we then have a **chromatic scale.** Note that the diatonic half steps remain constant. Enharmonic notes are also commonly substituted for double flat and double sharp notes.

Though sharps or naturals are normally used ascending and flats or naturals descending, the raised fourth degree is routinely used in both ascending and descending scales. Similarly, a lowered sixth scale degree is often substituted for a raised fifth. In minor, both altered and unaltered seventh degrees must be considered diatonic.

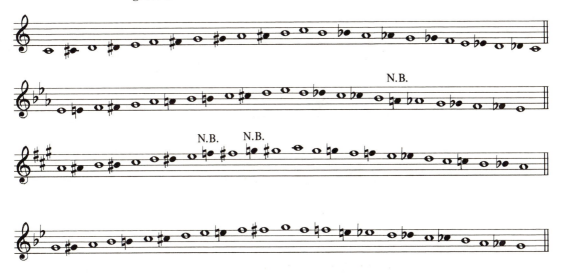

WRITTEN   1.   Add notes to make the following scales chromatic:
EXERCISES

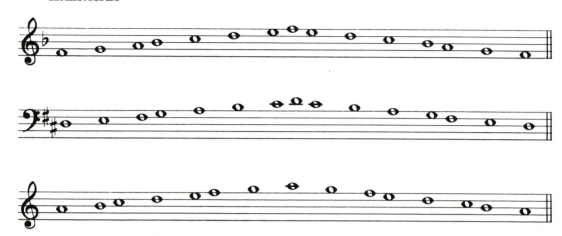

2.   Write chromatic scales, ascending and descending, starting on the given pitches:

MUSIC FOR   What are the key and mode of the following examples? Which pitches are
STUDY   diatonic? Which chromatic? Are the chromatic pitches neighbors or passing tones?

Remember that an accidental not in the key signature applies to every note in the measure on the same line or space. (The same note in another register would need its own accidental.) A barline cancels the accidental.

EXAMPLE 1.   WALTZ IN C MAJOR
Franz Schubert (1797–1828)

EXAMPLE 2.   MEXICAN HAT DANCE
Traditional

EXAMPLE 3.   "SWEET GENEVIEVE"
Traditional

Oh   Gen - e - vieve, Sweet Gen - e - vieve, The   days may come, The   days may go, But

still   the hands of   mem - 'ry weave The   bliss - ful dreams of   long   a - go.

EXAMPLE 4.   "BARNUM AND BAILEY'S FAVORITE" (TRIO)
Karl L. King (1891–1971)

EXAMPLE 5.   "HABANERA" FROM CARMEN
Georges Bizet (1838–1875)

L'a - mour est un oi -seau re - bel - le Qui nul   ne   peut___ ap - pri - voi -

ser,   Et c'est bien en vain qu'on l'ap -pel - le   S'il lui con - vient_ de_ re - fu - ser.

Translation: Love is a wild bird that none may tame, and one calls in vain . . .

EXAMPLE 6.   "PRELUDE TO A KISS"
Edward "Duke" Ellington (1889–1972)

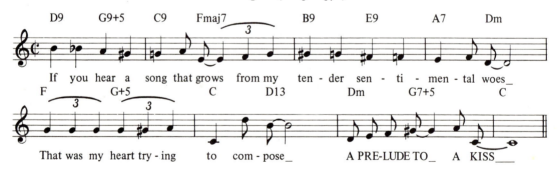

If   you hear a   song that grows from my   ten - der sen - ti - men - tal woes_

That was my heart try - ing   to   com - pose_   A PRE-LUDE TO_   A KISS___

Five

INTERVALS

WE MUST NOW consider the topic of intervals in greater depth. You will recall that any two pitches, considered in their relationship one to another, form what we call an *interval*. If the notes are played in succession, we have a **melodic interval;** if played together, a **harmonic interval.**

MELODIC INTERVALS

HARMONIC INTERVALS *

As you will recall, the interval's name or classification gives us two important items of information: (1) the *size* of the interval, by which we mean the number of scale degrees from one note to the other; and (2) *quality*, by which we mean the exact number of semitones contained in the interval.

---

*Observe the way the unison and second are notated when written as harmonic intervals (asterisked intervals).

The size of intervals is a general property and unproblematic. A note in relation to itself (the same letter-name in the same register) is a **unison** or **prime,** and is indicated by the number 1. Two notes a degree apart form a *second* (indicated by the number 2), notes three degrees distant form a *third* (indicated by a 3), and so on.

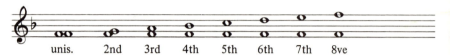

| unis. | 2nd | 3rd | 4th | 5th | 6th | 7th | 8ve |

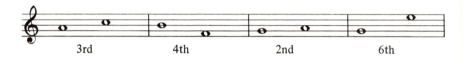

| 3rd | 4th | 2nd | 6th |

Quality is the more specific property that distinguishes intervals of notes with the same letter-names, and thus the same *size.*

SECONDS

We have already talked considerably about seconds. The half step is, in precise terms, a *minor second* (abbreviated m2). Minor in this sense means the small second. The whole step is a *major second* (abbreviated M2), major here meaning the large second. And we know there is a half-step difference between the two. We have also seen one instance of an *augmented second* (abbreviated A2), consisting of a step and a half. The augmented second is one half step larger than the major second. Let's compare all three:

| m2 | M2 | A2 | m2 | M2 | A2 | m2 | M2 | A2 |

Note that all three are considered to be seconds so long as the letter-names of the pitches are a degree apart. But the *quality* depends on the exact distance from one note to the other calculated in half steps.

EXERCISES   Review the computer drills on whole steps and half steps, as well as the written exercises for whole steps and half steps, from the previous chapter.

THIRDS

Because of their frequent occurrence in melodies, as well as their importance as the building blocks of chord structures, we should be very familiar with the qualities of thirds.

To review, the major third consists of two whole steps, and the minor third consists of a step and a half.

In our discussion of seconds above, we mentioned the augmented second. We can also create an *augmented third*, by either raising the upper note or lowering the lower note of any major third.

There is one other quality of third, and that is *diminished*. We create this quality by reducing a *minor third*, by lowering the upper note or raising the lower note.

Seconds may also be diminished. The resultant sound is enharmonically a unison. This written interval is rare.

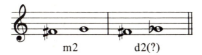

CHAPTER 5   INTERVALS

WRITTEN EXERCISES

1. Write major thirds *above* the given notes.

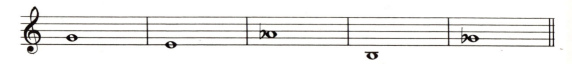

2. Write minor thirds *above* the given notes.

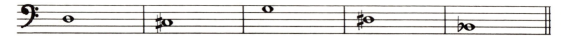

3. Write major thirds *below* the given notes.

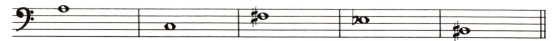

4. Write minor thirds *below* the given notes.

THE PERFECT INTERVALS

Unisons, fourths, fifths, and octaves are special cases. Why this is so can be seen if we compare the intervals formed by each degree of a major and natural minor scale with tonic:

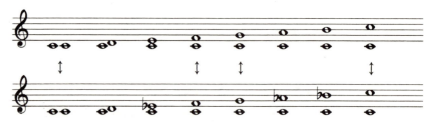

We see that the quality of the third, sixth, and seventh varies, but that the unison, fourth, fifth, and octave stay the same. (The second in this instance also stays the same, but as we have seen, seconds are like thirds in having a major and minor quality.)

Because of their immutability regarding scale formations, these intervals are called **perfect.** If we change the size of unisons, fourths, fifths, or octaves they become directly augmented or diminished. So unisons, fourths, fifths, and octaves are found basically only in three states—diminished, perfect, and augmented.

Unisons and octaves are, of course, the same pitch in either the same register or the next register. The augmented unison is the proper name for our by-now-familiar chromatic half step.

Augmented and diminished octaves are found occasionally. The diminished unison seems somewhat of an anomaly, but does exist (at least in the minds of music theorists!).

The perfect fourth consists of two whole steps plus a half step, or a major third plus a half step, or a minor third plus a whole step, or simply five half steps. We can calculate the quality of the fourths found in major and minor scales accordingly. Doing so, we will find a preponderance of perfect fourths, with only three important exceptions:

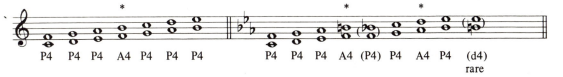

The asterisked fourths are all *augmented.* Since this interval consists of three whole steps, this interval is often termed a **tritone** (abbreviated TT), *tone* here being synonymous with whole step.

Here are the fifths found in both major and minor scale forms. The perfect fifth is a whole step larger than a perfect fourth, or can be calculated as a major third added to a minor third.

The diminished fifth (asterisked) is enharmonic to the augmented fourth, and is sometimes also called a tritone (TT).

SIXTHS AND SEVENTHS

We can calculate the qualities of these intervals either by counting half steps or adding smaller intervals together.

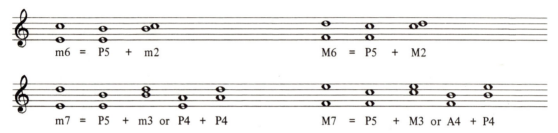

m6 = P5 + m2   M6 = P5 + M2

m7 = P5 + m3 or P4 + P4   M7 = P5 + M3 or A4 + P4

Here are sixths and sevenths in their scalar contexts:

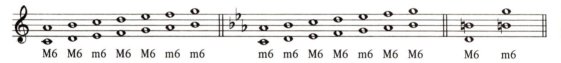

M6 M6 m6 M6 M6 m6 m6   m6 m6 M6 M6 m6 M6 M6   M6   m6

Sixths and sevenths, like seconds and thirds, come in four qualities (going from small to large): diminished, minor, major, and augmented.

d6   m6   M6   A6   d7   m7   M7   A7 (rare)

INVERSION OF INTERVALS

Calculating qualities of larger intervals can be cumbersome. There is a short cut, and it involves turning an interval "upside-down." By this we mean taking *one* of the notes and putting it either up or down an octave.

M3   m6   M3   m6

In our example, a major third has become a minor sixth.

There are two simple rules for determining the size and quality of inverted intervals:

1. The size of the new interval will always be the complement of nine. We can easily summarize this with a simple chart.

unisons	$\longleftrightarrow$	8ves	(1+8=9)
2nds	$\longleftrightarrow$	7ths	(2+7=9)
3rds	$\longleftrightarrow$	6ths	(3+6=9)
4ths	$\longleftrightarrow$	5ths	(4+5=9)

2. Perfect intervals remain perfect; major intervals become minor (and vice versa); augmented intervals become diminished (and vice versa).

Applying this rule to larger intervals, we first invert the interval and determine the quality of the inverted interval. Then, by applying the rules, we can quite simply determine the quality of the original interval.

1. Invert.
2. Determine quality (whole step plus half step = m3).
3. Apply rules: interval is M6.

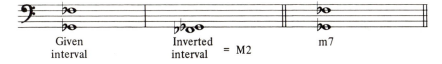

CHAPTER 5   INTERVALS
1. INTERVAL WRITING
    LEVEL 2—MAJOR, MINOR AND PERFECT INTERVALS ONLY
    LEVEL 3—SEVENTHS ONLY
2. INTERVAL SPELLING
    LEVEL 2—MAJOR, MINOR AND PERFECT INTERVALS ONLY
    LEVEL 3—SEVENTHS ONLY
3. INTERVAL RECOGNITION
    LEVEL 2—MAJOR, MINOR AND PERFECT INTERVALS ONLY
    LEVEL 3—SEVENTHS ONLY
4. INVERSION OF INTERVALS

WRITTEN
EXERCISES

1. Write perfect fourths *above* the given notes.

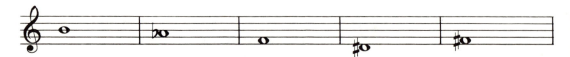

2. Write perfect fourths *below* the given notes.

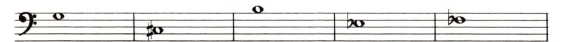

3. Invert the given interval. Then identify both intervals as to size and quality.

4. Analyze these intervals (size and quality) using the standard abbreviations.

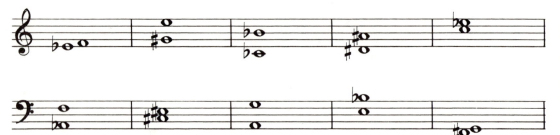

5. Analyze the melodic intervals in Examples 1, 3, 6, 7, and 9 in the Music for Study section on pages 149, 150, 152, 153, and 154.

6. Construct the indicated intervals *above* the given notes.

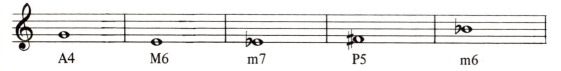

A4   M6   m7   P5   m6

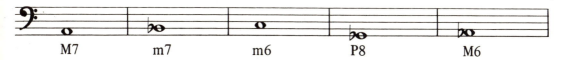

M7   m7   m6   P8   M6

7. Construct the indicated intervals *below* the given notes.

P5   M6   m6   M7   d5

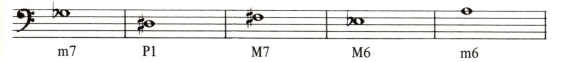

m7   P1   M7   M6   m6

COMPOUND INTERVALS

None of the intervals we have heretofore discussed have exceeded an octave in size, though it is quite common for larger intervals to occur. They are called **compound intervals**, and up to a tenth, they are commonly given their proper name:

M9   M10   m9   m10   A9   d10

Those over a tenth are often reduced to simple intervals for ease in identification:

P11 = P4   P12 = P5   m13 = m6

Compound intervals cannot, strictly speaking, be inverted.

CHAPTER 5   INTERVALS
   5. COMPOUND INTERVAL RECOGNITION

ALTERATION OF INTERVALS

As we have seen, we can change the quality of any interval by chromatically altering one or both of the notes. We can make the interval larger by either *raising* the upper note or *lowering* the lower note.

P4   A4   A4

Conversely, we can make the interval smaller by *lowering* the upper note or *raising* the lower note.

P5   d5   d5

Remember, major intervals first become minor and then diminished. Minor intervals first become major, then augmented.

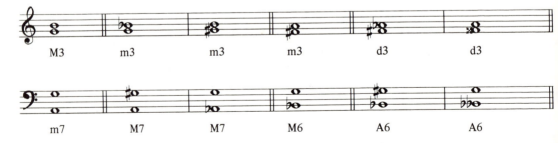

M3   m3   m3   m3   d3   d3

m7   M7   M7   M6   A6   A6

M7   m7   d7   d7   m2   M2   A2   A2

OTHER PROPERTIES OF INTERVALS

If both notes of an interval are found in a given scale or key, the interval is **diatonic.**

When one of the notes of an interval is foreign to a given scale or key, the interval is **chromatic.** Most augmented and diminished intervals will be chromatic, and it is not unusual for these chromatic intervals to contain both a sharp and a flat.

Intervals that contain enharmonic notes are naturally called **enharmonic** intervals. Among the more common are the diminished third and the major second, the minor third and the augmented second, the augmented fourth and diminished fifth, the augmented fifth and the minor sixth, the diminished seventh and the major sixth, and the augmented sixth and the minor seventh. Often, a useful check for the identification of chromatic intervals is to compare them to their enharmonic equivalents.

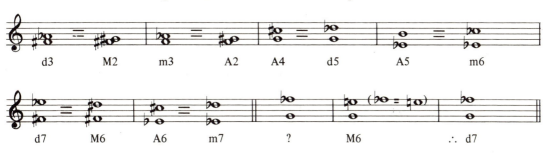

d3   M2   m3   A2   A4   d5   A5   m6

d7   M6   A6   m7   ?   M6   ∴ d7

It should be stressed that even though enharmonic intervals sound the same (at least on the piano), they are quite different in the way they are actually used.

Intervals are traditionally categorized as consonant or dissonant. **Consonant intervals** are considered relatively stable, **dissonant intervals** relatively unstable, requiring **resolution** to more consonant intervals. This aspect of intervals is critically dependent on context and changes with style and historical period. With most traditional tonal music, the following categorization can safely be assumed:

Consonances: all perfect unisons, fifths, and octaves; all major and minor thirds; all major and minor sixths.

Dissonances: all seconds and sevenths and all augmented and diminished intervals.

The perfect fourth may be consonant or dissonant, depending on how it is used.

CHAPTER 5   INTERVALS
1. INTERVAL WRITING—LEVEL 4—ALL QUALITIES OF SIMPLE INTERVALS
2. INTERVAL SPELLING—LEVEL 4—ALL QUALITIES OF SIMPLE INTERVALS
3. INTERVAL RECOGNITION—LEVEL 4—ALL QUALITIES OF SIMPLE INTERVALS

WRITTEN EXERCISES

1. Make the following major intervals *minor,* by altering one of the notes.

2. Make the following minor intervals *major,* by altering one of the notes.

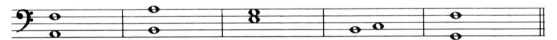

3. Make the following intervals *augmented.*

4. Make the following intervals *diminished.*

5. Analyze the following intervals, using the standard abbreviations.

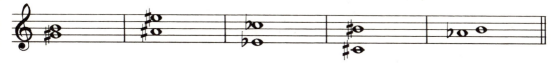

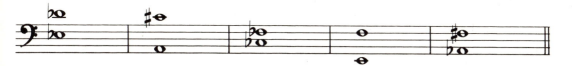

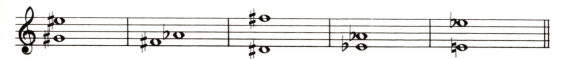

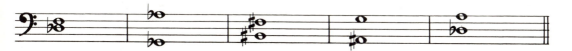

MUSIC FOR STUDY

Simple as it sounds, melodies use just three types of activity: (1) repetition of pitches; (2) stepwise (scalar) or conjunct motion; and (3) skips or disjunct motion. Most melodies strive for a balance of the three, with perhaps a slight preference for conjunct motion. Too much of any one type—but particularly repetition or skips—leads to dull and uninteresting melodies.

Listen to and then analyze the following melodies. Where do skips occur? Analyze those intervals. Are the skips large or small? What kind of melodic activity occurs prior to and following skips, particularly large skips?

EXAMPLE 1. "AMERICA, THE BEAUTIFUL"
Samuel A. Ward (1849–1903)

Oh   beau - ti - ful for   spa - cious skies, For am - ber waves of   grain,   For

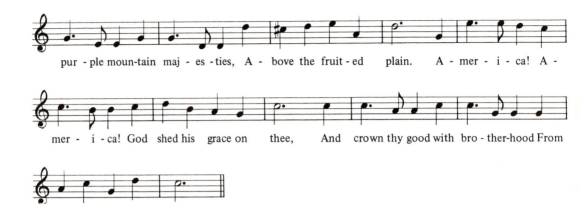

pur - ple moun-tain maj - es -ties, A - bove the fruit - ed   plain.   A - mer - i - ca! A -

mer - i - ca! God shed his   grace on   thee,   And   crown thy good with bro - ther-hood From

sea   to shin - ing   sea.

EXAMPLE 2.   PIANO CONCERTO IN B♭ MINOR, FIRST MOVEMENT
Peter Tchaikovsky (1840–1893)

EXAMPLE 3.   "THIS CAN'T BE LOVE"
Richard Rodgers (1902–1980)

This   can't be   love be - cause I   feel   so   well,_____   No

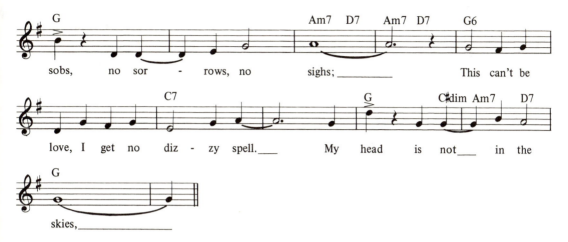

sobs,   no sor - rows, no   sighs;____   This can't be

love, I get no diz - zy spell.___ My head is not___ in the

skies,_____

Reprinted by permission of Hal Leonard Publishing Corporation.

EXAMPLE 4.   "TRY TO REMEMBER"
Harvey Schmidt (1929–   )

(Slowly, with tenderness)

1. Try To Re - mem-ber the kind of Sep-tem-ber when life was slow and

oh, so mel-low._ Try To Re - mem-ber the kind of Sep - tem-ber when

grass was green and grain was yel-low._ Try To Re - mem-ber the

kind of Sep - tem-ber when you were a ten - der and cal - low

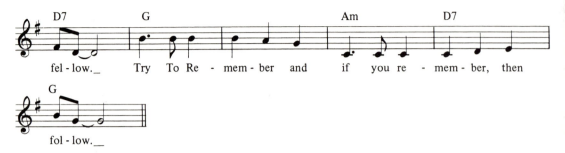

fel - low.__   Try To Re - mem - ber and   if   you re - mem - ber, then

fol - low.__

Reprinted by permission of Hal Leonard Publishing Corporation.

EXAMPLE 5.   "EDELWEISS"
Richard Rodgers (1902–1980)

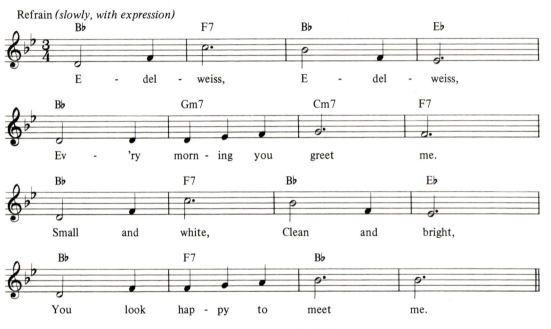

Refrain *(slowly, with expression)*

E - del - weiss,   E - del - weiss,

Ev - 'ry morn - ing you   greet   me.

Small   and   white,   Clean   and   bright,

You   look   hap - py   to   meet   me.

Reprinted by permission of Hal Leonard Publishing Corporation.

EXAMPLE 6.   GAVOTTE
Johann Sebastian Bach (1685–1750)

Consecutive leaps in the same direction generally outline triads, as in this example by Bach. You may wish to return to this example when you have studied Chapter 6.

The result of numerous large skips is often a **compound line.** In Example 7, a single disjunct line seems to form two conjunct lines when certain pitches are registrally related.

EXAMPLE 7.   THEME FROM *LOVE STORY*
Francis Lai

Music by Francis Lai. Lyric by Carl J. Sigman. © 1970, 1971 by Famous Music Corporation. All Rights Reserved. International Copyright Secured.

Here are the two lines that are implied:

Here are two other examples. As an exercise, write out the two implied lines. Remember that certain notes, such as the first G in the Bach example, may be common to both lines.

EXAMPLE 8.   MINUET IN G
Johann Sebastian Bach (1685–1750)

EXAMPLE 9.　"THE BLUE ROOM"
Richard Rodgers (1902–1980)

Six

CHORDS AND HARMONY

WE HAVE SEEN that if you play notes in succession you produce a series of melodic intervals, which form a melodic line. Similarly, if you play two notes simultaneously, you sound a harmonic interval. Three or more different pitches played simultaneously results in a **chord.** The following are all chords:

Most music consists of both a linear/horizontal (or melodic) dimension and a vertical (or harmonic) dimension. We typically think of an accompaniment, for example, as consisting of the chords that go along with the tune. But though these chords may be in the background, so to speak, the harmonic dimension is of crucial importance for helping to define the key and structure of the music.

For ease of discussion, we tend to talk about melody and harmony as if they were neat, separate phenomena, which they are not. Most melody tends toward clear harmonic implications, and any series of chords can, in fact, be shown to be a number of melodic lines occurring simultaneously. So in the discussion that follows, remember that a certain amount of overlapping is not only unavoidable but perhaps also desirable.

TRIADS

The chord structures most common to traditional tonal music are built out of thirds (and are so termed **tertian**). If we put two thirds together like this,

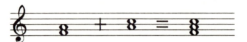

we have a **triad**. Triads, like intervals, have different qualities, and this is determined by the qualities of all the intervals contained in the triad. We name a triad according to its **root,** which is the note on which it is built, and its quality.

The other notes of the triad are named for the intervals they form with the root, namely the **third** and the **fifth.** We can now describe the four possible qualities of triads:

1. **Major:** M3 from root to third, m3 from third to fifth, and P5 from root to fifth. Major triads are indicated in chord symbols by a capital letter.

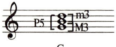

G

2. **Minor:** m3 from root to third, M3 from third to fifth, and P5 from root to fifth. Minor triads are indicated by a capital letter and a lowercase m.

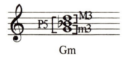

Gm

3. **Diminished:** m3 from root to third, m3 from third to fifth, and d5 from root to fifth. Indicated by a capital letter followed by a degree sign, or by the abbreviation dim.

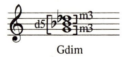

Gdim

4. **Augmented:** M3 from root to third, M3 from third to fifth, and A5 from root to fifth. Indicated by a capital letter and a plus sign.

G+

Of the four types, major and minor are found most frequently, diminished less frequently, and augmented the least.

CHAPTER 6   CHORDS AND HARMONY

1. TRIAD WRITING—ALL LEVELS
2. TRIAD SPELLING—ALL LEVELS
3. TRIAD RECOGNITION—ALL LEVELS

WRITTEN
EXERCISES

1. Write out the indicated triads on the treble staff, using accidentals only (no key signatures).
   Example:

A♭ major

a. E major

b. D minor

c. A♭ augmented

d. F minor

e. B diminished

f. A major

g. C minor

h. G diminished

i. D♭ major

j. D augmented

2. Write out the indicated triads on the bass staff, again using only accidentals.

a. B♭ major

f. C♯ minor

b. E minor

g. E♭ major

c. G♯ diminished

h. B♭ diminished

d. F♯ major

i. A♭ minor

e. C augmented

j. B augmented

3. Make the given triads *major* by adding the necessary accidental before one of the notes. No more than one note needs to be altered.

4. Make the given triads *minor.*

5. Make the given triads *augmented.*

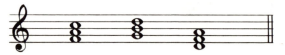

6. Make the given triads *diminished.*

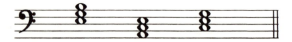

THE DOMINANT SEVENTH CHORD

If we add another third on top of a triad we have a seventh chord, so named for the interval from the root to the top note. We can build seventh chords on any pitch, and they will have varying qualities, just as triads do. We will examine all the qualities later. For now, there is one chord of special importance—the dominant seventh. This is a major triad with a minor seventh (indicated by a capital letter followed by the number 7) and is so called because it is the particular chord found built on the dominant in both major and minor.

G7

Remember this chord. You will encounter it quite frequently.

CHAPTER 6   CHORDS AND HARMONY

    4. DOMINANT SEVENTH WRITING
    5. DOMINANT SEVENTH SPELLING
    6. DOMINANT SEVENTH RECOGNITION

WRITTEN EXERCISES   Write dominant seventh chords on the treble staff, using only accidentals:

1. C7

2. E♭7

3. A7

4. D♭7

5. B7

MUSIC FOR STUDY

Triads seldom come as neatly arranged as the examples we have been seeing thus far. Even when the three notes of a triad are arranged together on a single staff, the order of the notes may vary from low to high.

SYMPHONY NO. 3, THIRD MOVEMENT
Ludwig Beethoven (1770–1827)

To determine the identity of the chord, we must rearrange the notes so that we have a series of thirds. The lowest note will then be the root.

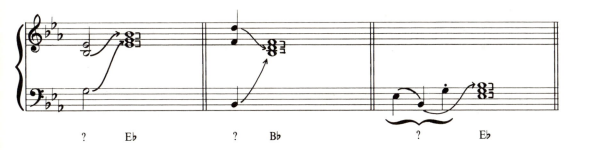

TEXTURE AND INVERSIONS

One very characteristic way of arranging chords is in **four-part harmony.** You may be familiar with this voicing from hymns and chorales. Because such pieces are written for four voices, but with predominantly three-note chords, one note must be duplicated. This is called a **doubling.** Here is a typical example of four-part harmony:

"OLD HUNDREDTH"
Louis Bourgeois (1510–1561)

Ho - ly   Ghost.

In order to identify the chords, we must again reduce the given tones to a series of thirds. This will tell us the root and allow us to determine the quality easily.

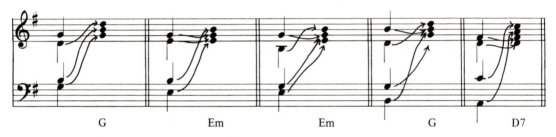

G   Em   Em   G   D7

In four-part harmony, we traditionally designate the various voices with separate stems and name each line according to its range—soprano, alto, tenor, and bass, going from highest to lowest. This is actually vocal-music nomenclature, but the terms are loosely applied to instrumental music as well.

This arrangement of the chords, or **texture,** allows us to see how the movement from one chord to another in any one voice actually forms a melodic line. This progression from chord to chord within a given line is called **voice leading,** and is a fundamental skill for all composers.

Even with both the melodic and the harmonic dimensions evident here, the balance is probably tipped toward the harmonic in this texture. This is due mostly to the **homorhythmic** character of the music. By this we mean all the voices are moving in basically the same rhythmic values. Lacking any significant rhythmic independence among the lines, the music will be perceived as predominantly a succession of chords; i.e., we hear the music *vertically.*

Now, let's look more closely at the lowest voice—the bass line. Much of the time, the bass has the root of the chord. We say that these chords are in **root position.**

(root)

But occasionally, the bass will have the *third* of the chord. We say that this chord is in **first inversion.**

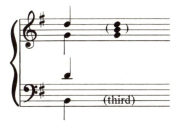

(third)

(We mustn't, however, confuse this use of the term inversion with that associated with intervals. They are related in a way, but the two usages should be kept distinct.) When the bass has the fifth, the chord is said to be in **second inversion.**

(fifth)

Inversions are used to give more melodic interest to the bass line. Important structural chords tend to be in root position, since this is the strongest and most easily identifiable position. Chords in inversion are often indicated in chord symbols like this: C/E bass, G/D bass, etc.

EXERCISES
1. Analyze the chords in the following chorale. Indicate with the standard letter symbols the root and quality of the chords. Indicate which chords are not in root position.

"STEAL AWAY"
Spiritual

2. Return to the example of "Old Hundredth" and identify the position of all the chords.

There is a seemingly infinite number of ways a composer can arrange a given chord. Some voicings may involve numerous duplications of chord tones in other registers:

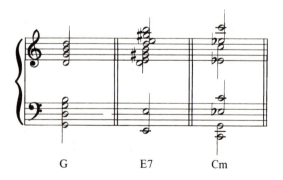

A chord may be broken up or **arpeggiated** within a single line:

A

Ddim

Gm

C#7

(Melodic figures that outline chords are called **arpeggios.**)

CHAPTER 6   CHORDS AND HARMONY
7.   CHORD RECOGNITION

EXERCISE   Identify the following chords presented in various arrangements. If necessary, reduce to thirds in close spacing, as before.

THE PRIMARY TRIADS

The study of harmony involves both an identification of the chords and some understanding of how and why those chords are used. A detailed study of chord relationships is well beyond the scope of this book, but some basic information can be helpfully applied to the music we routinely encounter, from the classics to the latest pop hit.

Just as certain beats or notes of a scale are more important than others, so certain chords within a key have special significance. They are the triads built on tonic, dominant, and subdominant, and they are often called the **primary triads.*** We will also include here the dominant seventh chord, since it occurs even more frequently than the dominant triad itself. For comparison, here are the primary triads in both G major and G minor. Note that the dominant chords in minor derive from the *harmonic* minor scale, with its raised seventh degree, and are accordingly major triad and dominant seventh respectively:

A surprising amount of music can be (and has been) written using only these chords.

The other chords are of lesser significance and are used primarily for variety:

The chords built on the leading tone (marked *) may conveniently be thought of as incomplete dominant sevenths. A major triad is frequently found built on the unaltered seventh scale degree in the minor mode (marked **).

---

*In traditional theory, chords are designated by the roman numeral of the scale degree of the root of the chord. This system is explained in Appendix Two.

NONCHORD TONES

We have seen that melodies typically consist of a balance of step and skip. Consecutive skips, or arpeggiations, naturally tend to suggest the underlying chords very clearly. But where the line moves by step, the relationship between the line and the chords becomes a bit more difficult.

Most of the time when there is a solo melodic line with a clearly separate accompaniment, the rhythms of the melody and accompaniment do not coincide, unlike the four-part harmony we saw earlier. The accompaniment may have arpeggios, with a fairly quick value, or off-beat chords.* Whatever the case, the rhythms of the melody will remain largely independent.

Moreover, we can talk about the rate at which chords change, or **harmonic rhythm.** In many styles, even rhythmically active melodies have *slow* harmonic rhythms, meaning few chord changes. A single chord played through several measures is not uncommon. Chords may change every measure, or may change within the measure, but still tend not to follow the rhythms of the melody itself.

For this reason, when a melody is moving by step against a single held chord, certain notes in the melody will obviously not belong to the chord. We call these notes **nonharmonic tones** or **nonchord tones.** We describe them in the manner in which they are approached and left. Here are the most common ones:

1. **Passing tone**—a note that moves from one chord tone to another by step. Several passing tones may occur in direct succession.

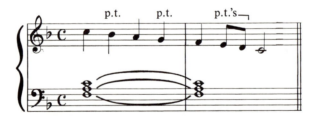

2. **Neighboring tone**—a note lying a step or half step above or below a chord tone. The single neighbor is quite common. A double neighbor also occurs frequently, and involves a skip from upper to lower neighbor or vice versa. This figure is also known as a **cambiata** or **changing tones.**

---

*For some examples, see below, and also in Chapter 8.

Neighbors may also be "freely" introduced. The free neighbor is also sometimes called an **unaccented appoggiatura.**

3. **Appoggiatura**—a note introduced by skip and resolved by step, generally in the opposite direction. Roughly translated, it means "leaning tone."

This is most typically found on a strong beat.

4. **Suspension**—a strong-beat nonchord tone that is repeated or tied across from a weak beat and resolved down by step.

5.   **Anticipation**—literally, a note that anticipates the coming chord tone.

6.   **Escape tone**—a tone that moves away by step from the basic direction of the line and then skips to the expected chord tone.

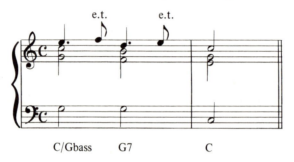

EXERCISES   Here are some melodies with simple accompaniments. Analyze the chords, then pick out and identify all the nonharmonic tones.

EXAMPLE 1.   SCHERZO
Franz Josef Haydn (1732–1809)

EXAMPLE 2.   WALTZ IN A MAJOR
Franz Schubert (1797–1828)

EXAMPLE 3.   "ROMANZE"
Felix Mendelssohn (1809–1847)

EXAMPLE 4. "ARABESQUE"
Johann Friedrich Bergmüller (1806–1874)

EXAMPLE 5.   "ROMANZE"
Ludwig Beethoven (1770–1827)

OTHER CHORDS: SEVENTH CHORDS

Seventh chords are found with a number of qualities. The most common one is that of the dominant seventh, which we have defined as a major triad with a minor seventh:

D7

The next most common quality is that of the **minor seventh chord.** This is a minor triad with a minor seventh, and is indicated by the letter of the root, small m, and the numeral 7. Minor seventh chords are found on supertonic, mediant, and submediant in the major mode; on subdominant and occasionally tonic in the minor mode. The seventh chord built on the dominant of any minor mode (and Mixolydian as well) will be a minor seventh. Use of this quality of the chord is one important contributor to the sound of modal music (that using the modes) as opposed to tonal music (that in either major or minor).

Dm7   Em7   Am7   Fm7   Cm7

A **major seventh chord** is defined as a major triad with a major seventh (indicated with maj7, as in the examples below). Major seventh chords are found on tonic and subdominant in major and on the mediant and submediant in minor.

Fmaj7   Cmaj7   A♭maj7   E♭maj7

The **half-diminished seventh chord** is a diminished triad with a minor seventh, and is indicated by the symbol ø7. This chord is found diatonically only on supertonic in minor and on the leading tone in major.

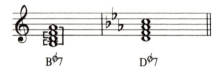

B^ø7   D^ø7

The fully-diminished seventh chord—most commonly called simply a **diminished seventh chord**—is a diminished triad with a diminished seventh, and is symbolized by the degree sign (°). This chord is found diatonically on the raised leading tone in minor, but is a very common chord in major as well. (See below under borrowed chords.)

F#°7

CHAPTER 6   CHORDS AND HARMONY

6.   DOMINANT SEVENTH RECOGNITION—NOTICE AND LISTEN TO THE CHORDS THAT ARE *NOT* DOMINANT SEVENTHS.

OTHER CHORDS: BORROWED CHORDS

We frequently find chords used that are not diatonic to the key. These chords always contain chromatically altered pitches and may conveniently be thought of as borrowed from another key.

Dominant sevenths are routinely found on almost any pitch. They generally resolve or progress to a triad whose root lies a fifth below, and they are analyzable as belonging to the key of that triad. For example, say we find a D7 in the key of C. This chord will almost always resolve to a G chord, and we can analyze this chord as the dominant seventh borrowed from the key of G.

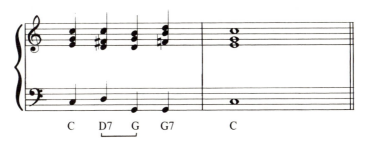

Here are other examples:

Chords are also frequently borrowed from the parallel mode. Common borrowings from minor to major are the seventh chords on scale degrees two and seven:

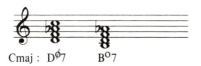

One common device is borrowing a major tonic triad for the final chord of a piece in minor. This raised third is called, for some unknown reason, a **piccardy third.**

EXERCISES   1.   Analyze the chords in the indicated measures. Which are diatonic and which are borrowed?

MINUET, K. 2
Wolfgang Amadeus Mozart (1756–1791)

10.___

2.   Identify all the chords in this example.

SYMPHONY NO. 4, THIRD MOVEMENT
Johannes Brahms (1833–1887)

OTHER CHORDS: SIXTH CHORDS

One chord frequently encountered in popular music is the triad with an added sixth. This chord is symbolized by the letter-name of the triad plus the numeral 6. The sixth may be added to either major or minor triads, but the sixth itself is virtually always a major sixth. This may require a chromatic alteration.

C6   Gm6

There is a certain ambiguity about this chord. We can get the same structure by putting a seventh chord in first inversion:

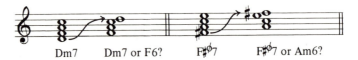

Dm7   Dm7 or F6?   F#ø7   F#ø7 or Am6?

Even the context will not always allow us to determine exactly which chord is intended. *Style* dictates that the sixth chord is to be expected in contemporary music, particularly pop and jazz, while the seventh chord is more likely to be the chord in Classical and Romantic music.

Both a sixth and a ninth may be found added to triads:

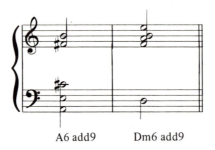

A6 add9   Dm6 add9

A given triad may appear superimposed over a bass note representing the root of another triad. Note the chord symbol.

$\frac{F}{Gbass}$

These chords are frequently encountered with **pedal tones**, which are long, sustained (or repeated) notes, generally in the bass, over which simple progressions occur.

EXERCISE   Write out the chords indicated by the chord symbols on these lead lines of popular songs.

THEME FROM *HOW THE WEST WAS WON*
Alfred Newman (1901–1970)

Rhythmically with great spirit (not too slow)

Prom - ised   land,   the   land   of plen - ty   rich and gold,

Here   came   dream-ers   with   bi - ble, fist and gun!   Bound for

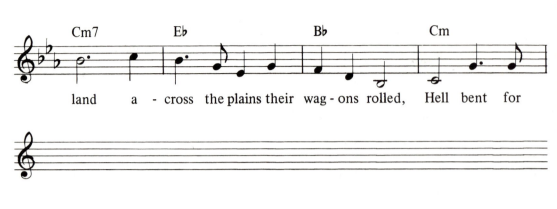

land   a - cross the plains their wag - ons rolled,   Hell   bent   for

leath - er;   That's How   The   West   Was   Won._____

"OVER THE RAINBOW"
Harold Arlen (1905–1986)

Some - where   o - ver the rain - bow   way   up

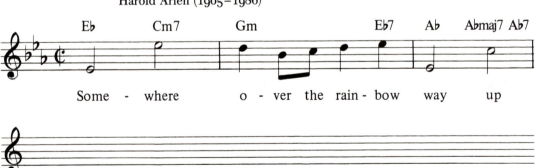

high,   There's   a   land that   I   heard   of

once   in   a   lull - a   -   by

Seven

SIMPLE FORMS

WE COME AT LAST to a consideration of musical form. As with almost any piece of art, **form** is that all-embracing term for the devices by which the artist composes, shapes, and organizes the raw material, which in music are the scales, intervals, chords, and rhythms that we have discussed.

Music, to have a convincing form, must have a sense of logical, directed motion from beginning to end. We also expect a certain coherence to the music—the sense that everything belongs. All good music, of whatever genre, seeks a balance between unity and variety, between tension and release, stability and change or flux. Lastly, the music must be clearly articulated; that is, we must know where the "seams" or divisions in the music occur.

PHRASES AND CADENCES

The basic "building block" of musical form is the **phrase.** A phrase may be defined as a complete musical thought—a gesture having a beginning, a middle, and an end. "Seams" or points of articulation occur at the ends of phrases, so this topic is of considerable importance.

Here are some familiar melodies with chord symbols, as you would find on a lead sheet or sheet music. Where do phrases seem to end? (Where is it logical to take a breath?) What chords are found at those points? What melodic pitches? What is the rhythmic value of the last note of a phrase?

EXAMPLE 1. " 'TIS SPRINGTIME"
Franz Süssmayer (1766–1803)

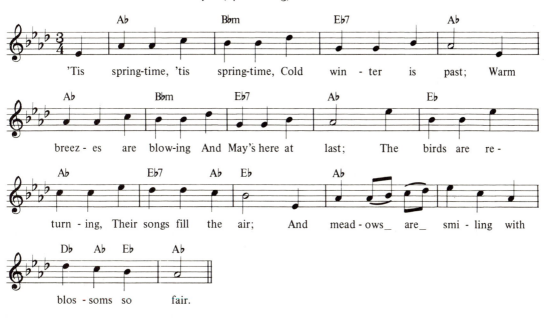

'Tis spring-time, 'tis spring-time, Cold win - ter is past; Warm
breez - es are blow-ing And May's here at last; The birds are re -
turn - ing, Their songs fill the air; And mead - ows_ are_ smi - ling with
blos - soms so fair.

EXAMPLE 2. "SOFTLY, SOFTLY"
Carl Maria von Weber (1786–1826)

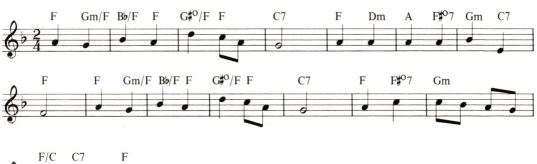

EXAMPLE 3.　"ALL BEAUTY WITHIN YOU"
Traditional Italian

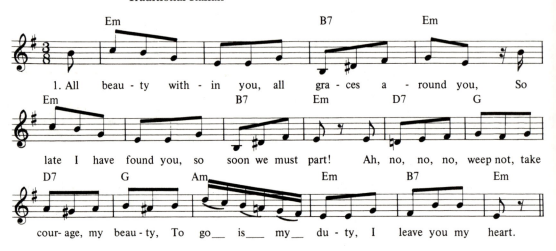

We normally expect to find one of two chords at a **cadence** (the term we apply to a phrase ending). The tonic chord gives us a stronger sense of finality or conclusion because of the inactive scale degrees it contains. Progressions of dominant to tonic at a phrase ending are called **authentic cadences.** Phrase endings on the dominant leave us feeling that the music wants to continue. For this reason, we call a cadence on dominant a **half cadence** or **semicadence.** In general terms, an authentic cadence could be characterized as *closed* or *terminal.* The half cadence, by contrast, would be characterized as *open* or *transient.* These are very loose categories. In the case of authentic cadences, a melody ending on tonic will sound more complete than a melody ending on the mediant or dominant. The former is termed a **perfect authentic cadence** (PAC) and the latter an **imperfect authentic cadence** (IAC). The IAC can be considered harmonically closed but at the same time melodically open!

Thinking back to our earlier discussions, we can now see that cadences are the result of the interaction of rhythm, melody, and harmony. We expect cadences to occur on strong beats, and we look for longer note values. Not every progression of dominant to tonic is a cadence, of course. Experience teaches us that phrases tend toward a norm of four measures, and we can always start by looking for cadences every fourth measure.

Two-measure phrases often are found with slow tempos, and three-measure phrases are not uncommon. Eight-measure phrases are likewise found in quick tempos. Irregular-length phrases very likely result from processes of phrase extension or expansion. In this case, the cadence will be very clear!

Points of structural articulation are also a product of the melodic content and design of the phrases. Much of the time, the phrases themselves will contain **motives.** A motive is a smaller structural unit, consisting of from one to three beats on average, which has a characteristic and readily recognizable rhythmic and melodic shape, but which does not seem to be complete or free-standing. Rhythmic motives often occur independently—that is, the same rhythmic pattern recurs, but without any systematic pitch conformities. As we have seen, rhythmic figures are crucial for establishing the meter, and as we will see, rhythmic patterning is the most usual method of unifying a series of phrases. Quite often the motive is germinal, and seems to "generate" all the music of the phrase. At other times, the phrase consists of two motivic ideas—one for the opening of the phrase, and a second idea for the cadence.

MUSIC FOR STUDY   The ways melody and harmony interact to establish points of articulation can be subtle, but are of vital significance. In the example below, find the cadence points. Don't forget the text. Are there motives?

"THE STREETS OF LAREDO"
Traditional Cowboy Song

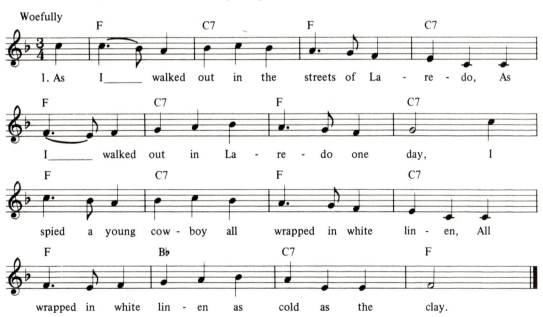

What we observe here, first of all, is that the cadences in measures 4 and 12 are relatively weaker than those in measures 8 and 16. There is a much greater degree of continuity of rhythmic motion. The long notes in measures 8 and 16 give a sense of pause in the musical flow. Now look at the beginnings of each phrase. Note the consistent use of the rhythmic motive ♩ | ♩. ♪ ♩ This helps to define the "seam" even where the cadence is weak. (This is even more important here, given the repetitious nature of the harmony.)

Phrase Relationships

Look again at the musical examples on pages 183–84. Pay particular attention to the melodic content of the various phrases. Do phrases share melodic material or are they different? What is the extent of the similarity or dissimilarity?

Form is a product of both cadence and the design or melodic relationships of the various phrases. The first phrase of a piece generally provides us the basis for later references, and most often ends with a relatively open cadence, suggesting more music to come.

Very often a first phrase will have the aspect of a question, achieved by a clearly open cadence, most usually a half cadence. The following phrase will then provide an answer, achieved by use of a clearly terminal cadence. This question–answer two-phrase structure is called a **period.** The question phrase is called the **antecedent** phrase and the answer phrase is called the **consequent.**

Many designs are possible. The two phrases may be **parallel**—i.e., share the same motives or melodic material. As a rule, only the beginnings of the phrases correspond, with the latter part changed to accommodate the different cadences. There may be slight variations even in the opening parts of the phrases. We can call the phrases parallel even if the material occurs in the second phrase at a different pitch level. (These periods are sometimes called **sequential** periods.)

Alternatively, the two phrases may be **contrasting**—i.e., the melodic material may be significantly different.

The design of phrases is indicated by small letters (a, b, c, etc.). Phrases with slight variations are indicated by prime signs along with the letter. For example, **a a′** indicates a parallel period.

Song Forms

There are two common forms that are typically encountered in songs.

The first possibility is AABA. The initial A phrases may be a repeated phrase or a period. The B phrase is virtually always open and the last A is a repetition or variation of the *second* A phrase. This is often expanded to 16 or 32 bars. The first 16 may be a repeated 8-bar period, then an 8-bar **bridge** or contrasting section, followed by a return of the first or second period. This is the form of many standard pop songs.

The other possibility is AAB, often called a **bar form.** The B is frequently extended to make it equal in length to both A's together.

EXAMPLES FOR THE STUDY OF FORM

EXAMPLE 1. "LULLABY"
Johannes Brahms (1833–1897)

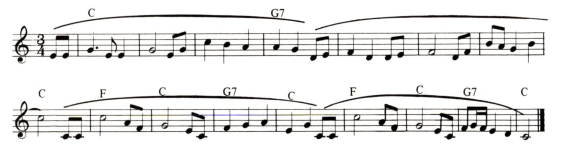

EXAMPLE 2. "WONDROUS LOVE"
Traditional

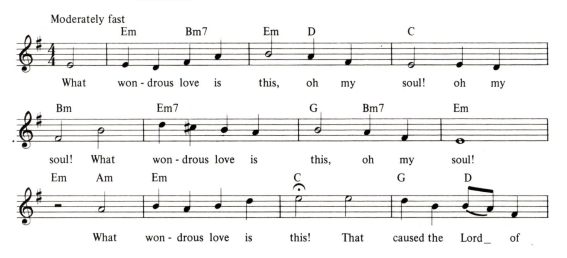

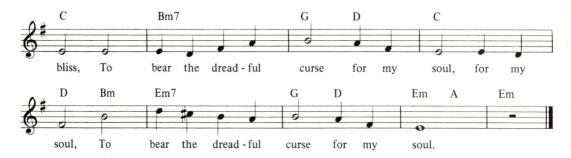

bliss, To bear the dread-ful curse for my soul, for my

soul, To bear the dread-ful curse for my soul.

EXAMPLE 3. "THE ASH GROVE"
Welsh Tune

1. Down yon-der green val-ley where stream-lets me- an - der, When twi-light is__ fad-ing I

pen-sive-ly rove, Or at the bright noon-tide in sol - i - tude wan-der A-

mid the dark shades of the lone-ly Ash Grove. 'Twas there while the_ black-bird was

joy - ful-ly_ sing-ing, I first met my_ dear one, the joy of my heart; A-

round us for glad-ness the blue-bells were ring-ing. Ah! then lit - tle__

thought I how soon we should part.

EXAMPLE 4.   "Susy, Little Susy"
Folksong

1. Su - sy, lit - tle Su - sy, now what is the news? The geese are go-ing
2. Su - sy, lit - tle Su - sy, some pen - nies I pray, To buy a lit-tle

bare - foot be - cause they've no shoes. The cob - bler has leath - er but
sup - per of sug - ar and whey. I'll sell my nice bed and go

no last has he, So he can-not make them the shoes, don't you see?
sleep on the straw, Feath - ers will not tic - kle and mice will not gnaw.

EXAMPLE 5.   CLARINET QUARTET, FOURTH MOVEMENT
Wolfgang Amadeus Mozart (1756–1791)

Allegretto

EXAMPLE 6.   "MORNING SONG"
Cornelius Gurlitt (1820–1901)

EXAMPLE 7.   "BAGATELLE"
Antonio Diabelli (1781–1858)

Harmonizing Melodies

It follows from what we have said that when harmonizing a given melody, we don't need to supply a chord for every note. We start by using the fewest chords, and then add additional chords for the sake of variety or added interest. The most important points to establish chords are at the beginnings and ends of phrases. Here are some examples for study and analysis.

"Believe Me, If All Those Endearing Young Charms"
Traditional

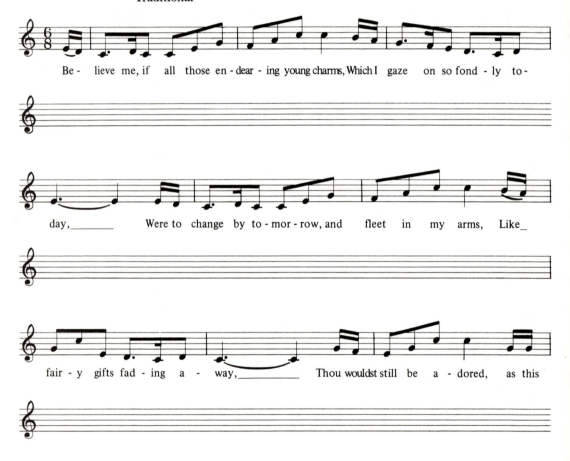

moment thou art, Let thy love - li - ness fade as it will,_____ And a-

round the dear ru - in, each wish of my heart, Would en-twine it - self ver - dant-ly still.___

"HOME ON THE RANGE"
Traditional American

Oh, give me a home where the buf - fa - lo roam, Where the

deer and the an - te - lope play; _____ Where sel - dom is

heard a dis - cour - ag - ing word, And the skies are not

cloud - y all day._____ Home, home on the

range,_____ Where the deer and the an - te - lope play;_____

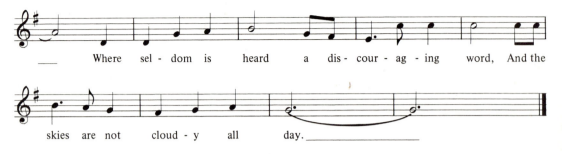

Where sel - dom is heard a dis - cour - ag - ing word, And the

skies are not cloud - y all day._____

CREATIVE EXERCISES   1.   Complete the following phrases with the indicated cadences:

         a.   End with a PAC.

         b.   End with an IAC.

         c.   End with an open cadence (half cadence or other).

     2.   Compose answering phrases to the following antecedents, as indicated:

         a.   Compose a parallel answer.

b.   Compose an answer using the same motive, but at a different pitch level.

c.   Compose a contrasting answer.

3.   Write original simple song forms, having the indicated designs:

   a.   A B A B′(C)

   b.   A A′ B A′

   c.   A A′ B(B′)

Eight

LOOKING AT MUSIC

WHILE LOOKING at a piece of music is indispensable for study, it can obviously (and thankfully) never replace *listening* to the music. Still, as we noted at the very beginning of this book, the written score is a very necessary link between the composer and the performer, and all musicians at some point must come to terms with the various skills of music reading. Let's summarize all that we've learned so far.

WHAT TO LOOK FOR IN A SCORE

1. *Format.* Is there a single staff, grand staff, or several staves grouped into systems?

2. *Basic information.* First, look at the *clef*, then the *key signature*, then the *meter signature*. Remember that the key signature may stand for either a major or a minor key.

   Next, look at the *tempo designation*. This will appear directly above the beginning of the first staff or system. The terms used here are often in Italian and were originally used to specify the character of the music.

   Unless stipulated by a metronome marking, tempo is an *interpretive* decision and is based on both the tempo designation and the meter and average note values.

   Other terms tell us about the character of the music, and here again, these terms are likely to be Italian. Among the most common are these:

appassionato—passionately, with great emotion

espressivo—expressively, with great feeling

maestoso—majestically

scherzando—playfully

These terms obviously indicate a certain manner or style of performance, and, like tempo terms, give the performer information that can't be communicated by the notes themselves. (Additional terms are defined in the Glossary.)

3. *"Road signs."* A double bar (‖) indicates a major structural division. This particular type of double bar (‖) is placed at the end of a composition.

    ‖: :‖ This sign means to repeat all the music within the double bars. Often different endings will be used and are designated like this:

    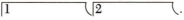
    ⌐1   ⌐2   ⌐.

    ✕   means repeat the previous measure.

     means repeat the previous two measures.

    / or // means to repeat the previous figure, generally a beat in duration.

    Here are other directions you will need to know:

    Dal Segno. (D.S.) Go back to the sign (𝄋).

    al Coda (⊕) Jump to the coda, indicated by the   ⊕   sign.

    al Fine. Play to the end or the point indicated by the word *Fine* (Italian for ending).

4. *Texture.* Most music has a principal melody—either an isolated solo line or the top voice of a chordal texture. Occasionally, a melodic line will be found in the bass, or in an inner voice. The melody itself will likely tell us the key, and may give us important clues as to the phrase structure. The melody will contain important motives and will establish the design of the music through the use of repetition, contrast, or recurrence.

    Harmonies are generally established by inner voices along with the bass. The harmonic progression confirms the key and the phrase structure. Sheet music for popular songs usually contains chord symbols above the vocal line, as a convenience for such instruments as the guitar.

    Very often, jazz musicians play from **lead sheets,** which give just the melodic line with the chord symbols. In this case, the written music serves only as a common basis for group improvisation.

5. *Form, shape, and design.* Once the key is established and the phrases have been located, we can think more broadly about the overall shape of the piece. Most music of even small dimension has the sense of moving to some climactic point and then winding down to the ending. This climax may be the highest point of the melodic line, the loudest point, the most intense or dissonant chord structure, or a combination of all of these.

Understanding the devices whereby the composer controls the flow of the music—now increasing, now relaxing the tension—is the ultimate goal of the study of music. We begin by *listening*—and by an initial awareness of our *reactions* to the music. Does it leave us exhilarated, or pensive, or sad, or joyful? Does it make us want to dance or suggest sober reflection?

Then we *look* at the music itself. What has caused our reaction? Is it the tempo, or the mode, or the character of the melody and/or the chord progressions? Likely it is some of all of these.

The study of music seeks to expand our awareness and thus appreciation of the complexities that go into a work of art. It may also open up new worlds for us, both as listeners and as performers, even if just amateur performances.

Music—as with the other arts—is an act of sharing, or communion, both with our fellow performers and between performer and audience, and ultimately between composer and listener. Through the remarkable language of music notation, we can share the thoughts of Bach or Beethoven or Lennon and McCartney—certainly the richest of heritages!

CHAPTER 8   LOOKING AT MUSIC

1. **MUSICAL TERMS—LEVEL 3—CHARACTER AND EXPRESSION INDICATIONS**

EXERCISES FOR
PRACTICE
IN READING
MUSIC

I. KUHLAU, OPUS 55, NO. 1

1. Identify the following terms and symbols:

p

f

sf

mf

$<$

poco a poco cresc.

dim.

espressivo

dolce

2. Explain the meaning of the meter signature.

3. What is the tempo of the piece? (Define the tempo designation.)

4. What is the initial key?

5. The key changes in measure 53 to _____ .

6. What scale is used in mm. 25–28 (right hand)?

7. Identify the chords in the following measures by placing the appropriate chord symbols in the music:

    1, 3, 17, 18, 19, 20, 21, 22, 25, 32, 33;
    53, 55, 56

8. In the first 16 bars, where do cadences probably occur? Identify them as to type.

    In bars 53–68, where do cadences occur? Identify them.

    What is the form of mm. 53–68?

9.   What happens beginning in bar 37?

10.   Is there a significant motive employed in this piece? If so, write it below:

SONATA, OPUS 55, NO. 1
Friedrich Kuhlau (1786–1832)

II.   BEETHOVEN, MINUET IN C

1.   Analyze the circled chords. What is the chord in mm. 9–12?

2.   Circle and identify the nonchord tones in the following measures: 4, 10, 17, 18, 19, 20, 28, 31.

3.   Define the following terms:

Moderato

D.C. al Fine

legato

4.   What is the form of bars 17–24?

MINUET IN C
Ludwig Beethoven (1770–1827)

legato   D.C. al Fine

III.   MINUET IN F
        Franz Josef Haydn (1732–1809)

        Discuss the overall form of this piece, considering both cadences and
        phrase design.

IV.   SCHERZO
Franz Josef Haydn (1732–1809)

Discuss the overall form of this piece, considering both cadences and phrase design.

V. BACH, MINUET IN G

This is an example of a two-voice composition—one voice in the right hand and the other in the left hand.

How does Bach keep the two voices separate and independent? How does he keep them equal? Identify the chords in mm. 1–6. How is the identity of these chords established?

Where do cadences occur? How are they established?

Are the phrases subdivided? Is there a significant motive employed?

What is the key of mm. 17–24? How is this new key established? What is the relationship of this key to G major?

What occurs beginning at measure 33?

Classify the meter signature. What is the unit of the beat? What is the most common note value? The next most common?

As was common practice in the Baroque Period (c. 1620–1750), Bach provides no tempo indication. Do the notes themselves suggest a tempo? If so, what would seem a reasonable metronome marking for the quarter note?

Is the pulse of this piece felt at the beat unit or at the background unit? Depending on the tempo, might the pulse be felt at the level of the single measure? Experiment with the effect of different tempos on your rhythmic perceptions.

MINUET IN G
Johann Sebastian Bach (1685–1750)

VI.   BARTÓK, "EVENING IN THE COUNTRY"

1.   Identify the following terms and symbols:

Lento

rubato

rit.

scherzando

Vivo

non rubato

Tempo I

2. What is the likely tonal center of this piece? State several reasons for your decision.

3. What scale is used in the first eight measures in the melody? (Disregard the chords here.) Write the scale below and identify it.

4. The first eight measures might also be said to be in what mode? (Consider *both* the melody and the chords!) Write out the scale, using the tonic you determined in question 2.

5. Identify the circled chords, using chord symbols. *Watch the clef signs!*

"EVENING IN THE COUNTRY"
Bela Bartók (1881–1945)

STANDARD CHORD PROGRESSIONS

HERE ARE several standard chord progressions in simple left-hand voicings for the piano. They may be used for class piano exercises, as the basis for improvisations or composition exercises, or as models for working out simple accompaniments to many of the melodies presented in the body of the book.

Any of these progressions may easily be transposed to other keys and used with other meters.

No. 1

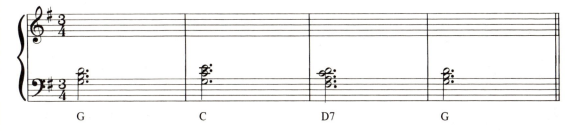

Here is the same progression in the parallel minor mode.

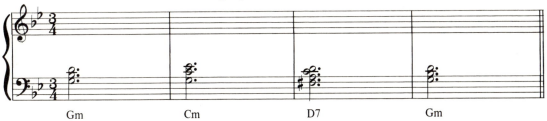

No. 2

This is the standard twelve-bar "blues" progression that plays such a prominant part in the history of jazz and popular music. You may want to compose or improvise some typical "walking" bass lines to accompany your tunes. / means to repeat the chord.

Appendix Two
ROMAN NUMERAL CHORD DESIGNATIONS

IN TRADITIONAL MUSIC THEORY, chords are designated by roman numerals. This system is both descriptive and analytic, in that it deals with both the chords *and* their integral relationships. The system is quite thorough but is somewhat limited in its application outside the realm of "common-practice" music—that music written in a functional, tonal idiom. Most basic theory courses concentrate on the music of the so-called common-practice period (c. 1730–1900), where roman numerals are most relevant. Theory courses dealing with contemporary music (including jazz and popular music) more often use letter designations for chords.

Since many students may want to go on to study traditional theory, here are the basics of the roman numeral system:

1. All chords are designated by the roman numeral corresponding to the scale degree of the root: tonic=I, dominant=V, etc.

2. Qualities of triads may be designated by using upper case for major, lower case for minor, and lower case with a degree sign for diminished. Here are the diatonic triads in major and minor, along with their roman numeral analyses:

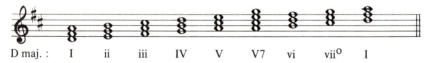

D maj. :   I   ii   iii   IV   V   V7   vi   vii°   I

D min. :   i   ii°   III   iv   V♯   V♯7   VI   vii°   i   VII

3. Inversions are indicated by using arabic numbers following the roman numeral:

I6   IV6   I$^6_4$

GLOSSARY

accelerando (accel.)—getting faster

accent—a feeling of stress or weight given to a beat or rhythmic value

accidental—a sign placed in front of a note to raise or lower the pitch

adagio—a slow tempo, faster than largo, slower than andante

agitato—agitated or excited

agogic accent—accent established by duration

allegretto—moderately fast, somewhat slower than allegro

allegro—quick, lively, bright; a fast tempo

anacrusis—an upbeat or pickup, i.e., one or more unstressed beats occurring prior to the initial downbeat of a phrase

andante—moderately slow, "walking" tempo

andantino—a little faster than andante

animato—animated, with life

anticipation—*see* nonharmonic tones

appassionata—passionately

appoggiatura—*see* nonharmonic tones

arpeggio—the tones of a chord sounded one after the other melodically

a tempo—in time; used to indicate a return to even time following an *accelerando, ritard,* or *tempo rubato*

background unit—that rhythmic value that represents the first or largest division of the beat

bar—a unit of division in music equivalent to the total of rhythmic values indicated by the meter signature

barline—a thin vertical line separating the music into measures

bass line—the lowest sounding voice

beam—a thick horizontal line connecting several flagged notes

beat—one of a series of regular and ongoing pulses or segments of musical time

216

ben—well, or marked, as in *ben marcato*, well accented

cadence—the ending of a phrase

calando—decreasing in tempo and loudness

cambiata—*see* nonharmonic tones

cantabile—in a singing style, lyrically

changing tones—*see* nonharmonic tones

chord—three or more pitches sounded simultaneously

chromatic—referring to notes that do not belong to the basic scale or tonality of the piece

clef—a sign used to denominate the lines and spaces of the staff. The treble clef places g1 on the second line, and the bass clef places f on the fourth line. There are also two C clefs: the alto clef places c1 on the third line, and the tenor clef places c1 on the fourth line.

compound meter—a meter in which the beat is divided into three equal background units

con—with, as in *con moto*, with motion; *con brio*, with fire or vigor; and *con forza*, with force

consonance—a feeling of stability, rest, or relaxation in music

crescendo (cresc.)—increasing in volume or loudness

Da Capo—return to the beginning

Dal Segno—go back to the sign 𝄋 and repeat

diatonic—referring to notes that belong to the basic scale or tonality of a piece

diminuendo (dim.)—decreasing in volume

dissonance—a feeling of instability or tension in music

dolce—sweetly, gently

doloroso—sadly

dot—a sign used to lengthen a note by half; a second dot adds half the value of the first dot

downbeat—the first beat of a measure

duple meter—a meter having two beats per measure

duplet—a sign used to indicate two equal values within a beat of compound meter

dynamic accent—accent established by volume or attack

dynamic—indication as to volume or loudness (e.g., *piano* and *forte*)

energico—with energy, vigorously

enharmonic—pitches or intervals that are spelled differently but are played on the same keys of the piano, e.g., F♯ and G♭

escape tone—*see* nonharmonic tones

espressione—expression

espressivo—expressively, with great feeling

fermata (⌢)—a sign used to indicate a hold or pause on a note or rest; also used occasionally to indicate the ends of phrases in chorales or hymns

Fine—the end; *al Fine*—to the end

forte (*f*)—loud

fortepiano (*fp*)—loud, then immediately soft

fortissimo (*ff*)—very loud

genre—type or style of music; often refers to the medium for which the piece is written

gracioso—gracefully

grave—seriously, indicating a slow tempo

great or grand staff—a treble and bass staff braced together and used for most keyboard music

half cadence—a cadence that suggests more music to come; an incomplete close, or transient phrase ending

harmony—the study of chords and chord relationships; the vertical dimension of music

hemiola—cross accents in simple triple or compound duple meters; the characteristic division of one meter appearing in or alternating with the other

homophonic—a texture characterized by an emphasis on the chordal dimension. Two common homophonic textures are chorale texture and melody with accompaniment.

imperfect authentic cadence—a cadence on tonic harmony, but with a pitch other than tonic in the melody

interval—any two notes considered in their relationship one to another

isorhythm—regularly recurring patterns of notes that contradict the given meter

largo—broad, very slow

ledger lines—lines the width of a notehead used to extend the staff both above and below

legato—connected notes played in an unbroken line

leggiero—lightly and delicately

lento—a slow tempo

l'istesso tempo—the same tempo

maestoso—majestically

marcato—marked, with strong accents

marziale—in a march style

measure—*see* bar

meno—less; with a dynamic mark, it means softer; *meno mosso*—slower, with less motion

meter—the organization of beats into recurring patterns of accent

meter signature—numbers placed at the beginning of the music to indicate the number and value of beat and/or background unit

mezzo—medium, as in *mezzo forte* (*mf*), moderately loud; *mezzo piano* (*mp*), moderately soft

middle C—c1; that C notated "midway" between the treble and bass staves of the grand staff

mode—the specific pattern of whole steps and half steps in a scale

moderato—moderately, a tempo neither fast nor slow

molto—much, as in *molto cresc.*, a great increase in volume

morendo—dying away, fading

motive—a brief musical idea having a definite melodic and/or harmonic character

moto—motion

neighboring tone—*see* nonharmonic tones

non—not, as in *non dim.*, no decrease in volume

nonharmonic (nonchord) tones—
melodic pitches that do not belong to the underlying harmony.
Here are the most common:
anticipation—a metrically weak
note that anticipates the following chord
appoggiatura—a metrically
strong note introduced by skip
and resolved by step in the
opposite direction
cambiata, changing tone—a
metrically weak note introduced by skip and resolved by
step, an unaccented appoggiatura; the term also used for
a double neighboring tone
escape tone—a metrically weak
note that is introduced by step
and resolved by skip
neighboring tone—a note lying a
step above or below a chord tone
and returning to the same tone,
generally metrically weaker than
the chord tone
passing tone—a tone that moves
stepwise from one chord tone to
another, generally metrically
weak; accented passing tones are
common in descending lines
with much the same character as
appoggiaturas
suspension—a metrically strong
note that is prepared as a chord
tone of the previous chord and
subsequently resolves stepwise
downward
note—a symbol designating a particular rhythmic value and,
when placed on a staff, a particular pitch

octava (8ᵛᵃ)—indicating notes to be
played one octave (eight steps)
higher or lower (*octava bassa*)

passing tone—*see* nonharmonic
tones
pedal tone—a generally long note,
most often in the bass, against
which harmonic progressions
occur
perfect authentic cadence—a cadence on tonic harmony with
the tonic pitch in the melody
pesante—heavily
pianissimo (pp)—very soft
piano (p)—soft
piccardy third—a raised third in a
final cadential chord in minor
pickup—a note (or notes) occurring
prior to the initial downbeat of
a phrase
pitch—the relative highness or
lowness of a musical sound, a
product of the speed of the
vibrations in the sound; indicated by the placement of notes
on the staff
più—more; *più f*, louder; *più
mosso*—faster
plagal cadence—a terminal cadence
progressing from subdominant
to tonic harmony
poco—a little; *poco a poco*—
gradually
polyphony—a texture combining several independent
melodic lines
presto—very fast

register—the relative placement of
pitches in the gamut from low
to high. A given register consists of the octave from one C to
the next.
rest—a symbol indicating a specific
duration of silence

rhythm—the various durations or note values found in a piece of music

rinforzando—reinforced, suddenly stressed

ritard (rit.)—a slowing of the tempo

ritardando—gradually slowing

ritenuto—a holding back, immediately slower

rubato—a free or flexible tempo

scale—the pitches used in a given piece of music, ordered from high to low. Diatonic scales include the major scale, the various minor scales, the modes, and the pentatonic scale. The chromatic scale contains all the pitches commonly used in tonal music.

scherzando, scherzino—capriciously, in a light playful manner

score—the written music

secco—dry, short, and crisp

semplice—simply

sempre—always

sforzando (*sf, sfz*)—with force or an explosive accent

simple meter—a meter in which the beat is divided into two equal background units

slur—a curved line indicating a legato articulation; also used as a phrase mark

sostenuto—sustained

sotto voce—in an undertone

spiritoso—with spirit or verve

staccato—detached, separate

staff—parallel lines and spaces used in music to indicate pitches; the modern staff consists of five lines (and four spaces)

stringendo—accelerating markedly

subito—suddenly

suspension—*see* nonharmonic tones

syncopation—the displacement of the normal patterns of metric accent

system—a number of staves braced together

tempo—the rate, pace, or relative speed of the beat

tenuto—held out full length, or even slightly longer

texture—the various elements of music—melody, harmony, bass line, accompaniment, etc.—and their mutual relationships

tie—a slightly curved line joining two notes into a single rhythmic value

timbre—the tone colors found in music

tranquillo—tranquilly, peacefully, restfully

triple meter—a meter having three beats per measure

triplet—a sign used to indicate three equal values within the beat of a simple meter; also used in any situation where three notes are to be played in the time of two notes

una corda—with the soft pedal of the piano

upbeat—the beat immediately preceding the initial downbeat; the last beat in a measure; the unaccented beats in a measure

vivace—very lively, fast tempo

vivo—lively

Indexes

COMPOSERS

CLASSIC SONGS (*All Single Line*)*

*CS: chord symbols

CHORALES AND HYMNS

FOLK SONGS*

POPULAR SONGS*

SINGLE-LINE INSTRUMENTAL EXAMPLES

---

*CS: chord symbols   **SL**: single line   **A**: accompaniment

Simple Piano Pieces

Topics